JUSTICE DENIED

HOWELL WOLTZ

JUSTICE DENIED

The United States vs. the People

WOLTZ MEDIA CORPORATION
WILMINGTON, DELAWARE

Woltz Media Corporation
Wilmington, Delaware

Published in the United States of America
by Woltz Media Corporation
First printing July 2010

Cover design and sculpture, *Homefront* copyright © 2013
by Rob Calvert. All rights reserved.
Photo on back cover by David Rosen.

Discounts are available to your company, non-profit or educational
institution for reselling and/or educational purposes.

For more information, please contact the publisher at:
Woltz Media Corporation, PO Box 2216, Advance, NC 27006
Email: Howell@WoltzMedia.com

For my mother, Patricia Gwyn Woltz
(1925 - 2011)

CONTENTS

ACKNOWLEDGMENTS

This book is dedicated to the men and women of the United States of America who are working tirelessly to restore our government and its judiciary to the constitutional and legal boundaries from which both have escaped.

The debt to those who made this book possible under incredible hardships and even danger is impossible to repay. I am forever grateful to you all, and wish you could be recognized by name without putting you in unnecessary peril.

Ruby Lambert, age 93, chief editor of this book and my father's Executive Assistant for twenty-nine years, gave me permission to do so. She said, "At my age, they can just come on and get me."

FOREWARD

By ARTHUR P. STRICKLAND
Attorney, former United States Magistrate Judge

I learned Howell's story over dinner one night in 2008 through a member of his family. I am an attorney, a former Federal Law Clerk and a United States Federal Magistrate Judge. I have practiced law for over thirty years in State and Federal courts. What I heard initially struck me as exaggerated at best and preposterous at worst.

Somewhat reluctantly, I agreed to go to the Federal prison where Howell was housed in Beaver, West Virginia to see him in person. He claimed to have been convicted and sentenced as a "sole conspirator" despite spending large sums of money on well-known attorneys.

As a legal and Constitutional matter, and relevant to Howell's case, a court's jurisdiction cannot be conferred or usurped. Either a court has it or it does not, and no court foreign to the court of jurisdiction can rule in a case until it has been fully adjudicated by the original court. Howell contended that though he had been charged in the Western District North Carolina Court, he had been adjudicated and sentenced in an Eastern District Court, which did not have jurisdiction to do so, after being released on bond by the court of jurisdiction.

Howell also contended that he had ineffective assistance of counsel (his attorneys had not followed his direction to challenge these issues and made misrepresentations to him) and when he did finally plead guilty it was under duress to the point that it was an involuntary plea. That plea was also held in a court foreign to that of jurisdiction, which would in fact, have made that plea void under Rule 20 of the Federal Rules of Procedure and 18 U.S.C. §3234, as well as the Sixth Amendment to the U.S. Constitution.

Still doubtful and admittedly not wanting to believe such could happen, I returned to Howell's prison with witnesses to the events, including his brother and an attorney, who had tried to help him at one point. I thereafter visited him several times and documented many of the allegations he was making.

I was not licensed in North Carolina where he was convicted or in West Virginia where he was incarcerated and thus could not represent him in his post-conviction efforts. I did try to help him to the extent I could from afar. By 2009, convinced that Howell had identified committed injustices, I began writing the Chief Judge of the Federal District Court in North Carolina where the alleged violations had occurred. I asked the judge to review Howell's case in the interest of justice. There was no response to those requests. At a minimum Howell had raised substantial issues and deserved a hearing at which those issues could be addressed.

In spite of this, Howell served an 87-month sentence in Federal prison. Every Federal court with the authority to address his allegations either ignored them or simply dismissed them without inquiry beyond his guilty plea.

Throughout all of Howell's appeals, issues of jurisdiction, ineffective assistance of counsel and the involuntariness of his guilty plea have never been fairly addressed. What this book points out is the institutional corruption that has now seeped into the criminal justice system. Overwhelmingly, criminal cases are disposed of by plea bargains, which can only be called *bargains* in the loosest sense of the word. The deck is very much stacked in favor of the prosecutors as will become evident to the reader as one sees how Howell's case was managed, and the courts, which should be arbitrators of justice, have taken on an increasingly ministerial role in rubber-stamping what is handed to them by the prosecution.

The Bill of Rights is designed to "level the playing field" in criminal prosecutions. It is thwarted in many cases for the same reasons it was against Howell and his wife, as victims of the system.

To that end, I endorse this book and Howell's efforts to do justice.

Arthur P. Strickland, Attorney, Roanoke, VA
January 14, 2013

Federal Judicial Districts: North Carolina

A **Federal judicial district** is the geographic
organization of Federal general trial courts in the
United States.

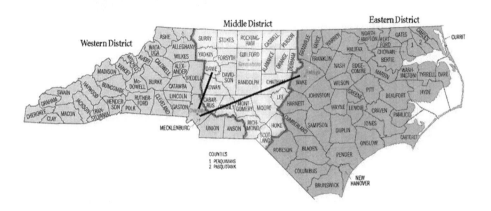

Howell Woltz was arrested in the Middle District, arraigned in the Western District and adjudicated in the Eastern District, in violation of Federal law and the United States Constitution (Amendment Six).

(Map provided by http://www.fedstats.gov/fjd/37fjd.html.)

"It has long been my opinion. And I have never shrunk from its expression…that the germ of dissolution of our Federal Government is in the constitution of the Federal Judiciary—an irresponsible body (for impeachment is scarcely a scare-crow), working like gravity by night and by day, gaining a little today and a little tomorrow, and advancing its noiseless step like a thief over the field of jurisdiction until all shall be usurped from the States and the government be consolidated into one. To this I am opposed."

Thomas Jefferson to Charles Hammond, 1821. ME 15:331

CHAPTER 1

THE WAY HOME

April 14, 2006

T he familiar scenery scrolled by as I left the Charlotte-Douglas International Airport and headed north on I-77. I must have made the drive a thousand times and would make it again a few days later to pick up the family from Nassau where we were living at the time. I ran a small trust company there, and we were coming back to the farm for a vacation during our son's Spring Break.

I'd been commuting in and out of the country through the portal of Charlotte for most of my adult life. The city went from a nondescript industrial hub when, as a child, I first accompanied my father on business, to becoming one of the banking capitals of the world by 2006. The new billboards at the airport exit welcomed me home in seven languages. Charlotte was all grown up.

I had been in New York working with institutional partners of our company the week before and celebrated the induction of a business partner into the Trader's Hall of Fame. After three days of this, I could not wait to tear off my shoes and sink into some North Carolina red clay.

No matter where I lived during my 52 years, North Carolina was still home. My mother's family was in the region since the 1600s.

Through hard work they carved a living out of its mountains. My father's ancestors came from Germany two centuries later and did the same in the state's lowlands. Our roots were deep in that clay, and I was proud of it.

Too many moons passed since our last visit home. I was earning a doctorate degree in Nassau, taking classes on weekends for nine months. Between work and school, this was the first opportunity in almost a year to be at the farm. I wanted everything at the old place working before the family arrived. My wife, Vernice, and our youngest, John, were coming by plane in two days. John's schoolmate, Stewart, was coming with them, and I wanted the cabin clean and presentable. Our two older children, Kate and Christopher, were away at school, but we hoped to see them as well.

I missed the changes of seasons living in the Caribbean. Now April, the prettiest time of the year, North Carolina was in full bloom. Turning east on I-40, I could smell the unique springtime scents of state and home. Leaving the highway and driving into our little borough of Advance always gave me a thrill. So many wonderful memories surrounded our times there.

Driving by the small Post Office reminded me of the Saturday mornings of previous years when John and I worked his lemonade stand before we moved to The Bahamas. Every Friday night, we would make up two large containers of lemonade using his special recipe, which included pure spring water, raw turbinado sugar, and the best lemons he could find. He would prepare his change box, tally up his expenses, and pack the table and sign in the Jeep for the next morning's commerce. I loved those days. John was a special child. I loved our older two children equally as much, but John was my last, and I treasured every moment with him.

My schedule in The Bahamas was arranged so we could spend time together. By starting work early in the morning, I could be with him after school. Almost every afternoon we paddled to the reef in our inflatable kayak and spearfished, rode our bikes along the beach, or played chess, then did our homework. Those were wonderful days.

I rolled down the window of the rental car as I turned onto the gravel road to the farm and smelled the heavenly scent of cherry laurel and honey locust blossoms wafting up from the cabin. It was good to be home.

A few days later, I picked up the family at the airport, and our vacation began in earnest. The bass were biting, and the stress of life unknotted itself as we settled in for the week. More idyllic setting and circumstances would be hard to find

Only one business activity was scheduled. Two years earlier, our company filed a Suspicious Activity Report with the Central Bank of The Bahamas regarding a trust account set up by former North Carolina U.S. Attorney, Samuel T. Currin, on behalf of his clients. The current U.S. Attorney and FBI had somehow received a copy of the report and wanted to discuss what I knew about Mr. Currin's activities. I scheduled a meeting with them at the U.S. Attorney's office in Charlotte.

One quick trip there on the morning of April 18 to do my civic duty would leave the rest of the trip free for family and fun.

CHAPTER 2

THE FEDERAL BUREAU OF INVESTIGATION

"The United States wins its case whenever justice is done one of its citizens in the courts."

Inscription on the wall of U.S. Department of Justice, Washington, D.C.

April 18, 2006 7:38 a.m. – Middle District of North Carolina

It was a soggy and foggy morning as I left the farm for the meeting in Charlotte. The man they wanted to discuss, Samuel Currin, was under investigation for financial fraud. His law firm was briefly a customer of our trust company from 2003-2005. Our firm had offices in The Bahamas, British Anguilla, and St. Lucia, and though not subject to U.S. law, we meticulously followed it when dealing with U.S. clients. Our rules required all clients, U.S. or not, to provide the firm with the source of any funds sent to the firm, a sworn statement as to their legal origin, and the payment of required taxes to their home nation.

After three requests, Sam Currin chose not to provide the source of funds we had received. Red flags went up with our due diligence department. In cases where clients did not provide such information, it was our policy to no longer accept their business. Mr. Currin was informed to move his business elsewhere. I filed an S.A.R. (Suspicious Activity Report) with the Central Bank. End of story, or so I thought.

As a regulated financial firm, we were required to assist any government investigation, if asked, so I agreed to meet with FBI agent Doug Curran and an assistant U.S. Attorney, Matthew Martens, to discuss our report. I remember wondering if FBI agent Doug *Curran* and his target, former prosecutor, Sam *Currin*, may be distantly related. I also recall being somewhat excited about meeting a real, live agent of the modern FBI. As a young boy I studied the organization and at one point considered pursuing law or accounting, which in those days was a requirement of becoming an agent.

I learned about the FBI's creation and the huge political battle this caused in 1907. Congress ultimately refused to authorize the new agency, based on the argument there was no constitutional provision for a national police force. Using the now common *executive order*, President Roosevelt created the bureau over the objections of Congress.

My mother instilled her love of reading early on and kept us well stocked with history books and classics where more or less any such topic could be researched. Growing up in the country, our entertainments were mostly outdoors. We rode horses, worked on the farm, played cowboys and Indians (I always wanted to be an Indian), and were Boy Scouts. My brothers Jim and Thomas and I became Eagle Scouts like our father. There were not many indoor entertainments besides reading, and I soaked up everything I could get my hands on when the opportunity came. Our nation's history was my favorite, which led to a lifetime study of the U.S. Constitution and our nation's founders.

I am convinced we have the best system of government possible for a nation such as ours, but disturbed we no longer live by its design. Our Constitution is a piece of timeless art. Its primary author, James Madison, was not a lawyer, yet he created what is, in my opinion, a most remarkable legal document. Its beauty and nuance continue to amaze when read today. I thought the events scheduled in Charlotte would be of particular interest, providing a firsthand view of how our system actually worked. All I knew was government's target of prosecution, former U.S. Attorney, Sam Currin, would not give our staff information on the source of funds. We were unaware how those funds were earned as the report stated. This made me wonder why they wanted to talk in the first place. All I could tell them was I knew little, which should not take long.

This suited me fine. The fog would burn off soon, and the kids and I could be fishing by noon.

CHAPTER 3

THE FBI RUINS MY DAY

"Society wins not only when the guilty are convicted but when criminal trials are fair: our system of the administration of justice suffers when any accused is treated unfairly."

**Brady v. Maryland, 373 US 83,
10 L.Ed.2d 215, 83 S.Ct. 1194 (1963)**

April 18, 2006 7:45 a.m. – Middle District of North Carolina

The U.S. Attorney's Office in the Western District of North Carolina had a slightly different plan for me on that spring morning.

As I eased past one of the farm buildings, I noticed a white SUV parked behind it. Two people, a man and a woman, were sitting inside. It seemed too early for the fox hunting "Tally-Ho" crowd who leased the farm. I had no idea who these people were or why they were there.

The SUV pulled in behind me. If it contained young lovers, I clearly ruined their moment. The car stayed back until I topped the hill where our lane comes to the state road, and then closed in. I saw several cars at the end of our road, including two cruisers from the local sheriff's department. Someone must have gotten him or herself in trouble. I then saw the people had bright yellow *FBI* letters on their parkas.

Why would they be here? I was on my way to Charlotte to meet them.

I rolled down the window of the rental car. Agent Doug Curran, one of the men I was to meet in Charlotte, was at the end of the road.

"I'm on my way to meet you, Mr. Curran," I said, "Does this mean the plans have changed?"

"We decided to do it a little differently," said the agent, "Would you step out of the vehicle with your hands up?" It was phrased like a question, but certainly didn't sound like one the way he said it.

I noticed at least seven Glock semi-automatics, plus whatever the Davie County deputies had in their holsters, all within a few feet of my head and did as he asked.

They stripped me of my jacket, wallet, cash, Swiss Army knife, Blackberry phone, and belt, then handcuffed me from behind, and shoved me headlong into the backseat of Agent Curran's sedan. The neighbors who drove by gawked at the scene like something from a B-grade cop show.

Agent Curran played good cop *and* bad cop. The rest of the agents drank coffee and let their adrenalin dissipate after the dangerous capture of the man who was already en route to their office. I volunteered to come and assist them, yet here I was like a criminal sitting handcuffed in the back of an FBI sedan. Agent Curran offered to return the rental car to my house. He asked for the keypad code to the electronic gate.

I was alarmed by the thought. Could this be construed as giving them permission to enter the house, which would terrify my wife and the kids?

"Leave the car at the gate," I said.

"Don't you want your wife to know it's there and tell her what happened so she won't worry?"

He dialed the home number and placed the Blackberry to my ear.

"Hello," my wife's sleepy voice said.

"The FBI was waiting at the end of the road to arrest me. They're bringing the car down now."

"Why? What for?" The shrieking voice was now fully alert.

"I have no idea. Just meet them at the gate and get the keys, OK? Try to find Doug Hanna when you get back to the house and tell him what happened."

Doug Hanna was a lawyer with Womble, Carlyle, Sandridge & Rice. He was on his way to Charlotte from Raleigh, North Carolina for the scheduled meeting. His assistance had been helpful when our firm uncovered and reported a securities fraud to the S.E.C. No one at the Commission responded, so we sent the information to the Office of the U.S. Attorney in Charlotte through Doug's law firm. This too was to be reviewed at the same meeting.

After the call, Agent Curran, smiled and said, "I'd be happy to take the car down to the house so she doesn't have to walk up to the gate to get the keys, if you'll just give me the code."

I wasn't sure I wanted this gang showing up on the porch with their semi-automatics, traumatizing my family.

"I don't think so, Mr. Curran. I'd rather just have you meet her at the gate."

A few minutes later his agents returned with another captive. Out of the back seat of a government sedan emerged the mother of my children, hair askew, glasses on, (no time for contacts), dressed in a jean skirt wrapped around a long t-shirt nightgown. From what little could be seen of her posture, I saw a raging fire.

She was frisked then shoved headfirst in the back seat. Agent Curran returned wearing a smirk.

I asked, "Are you aware you just left two children asleep in the house? They will have no idea what happened to us when they wake up."

"That's not my problem. My orders are to get you to an arraignment, and that's all I'm concerned with."

Arraignment? I hadn't even seen a warrant for my arrest (and haven't to this day). I was blown away. "You mean leaving two little boys, ages eleven and twelve, alone in a house way out here, after you've kidnapped both their parents, is not your responsibility?

"Would you let me call someone to come get them?"

"Who?"

"Our local Chief of Police, Robert Cook," I replied. In addition to being Chief, Robert was also my best friend and godfather to Chris. We had dinner at his house the night before.

Curran dialed Robert's home on the Blackberry, and held it to my ear.

"Robert, this is Howell. The FBI has taken me into custody, Vernice also. I don't know for what or why, but the boys are asleep in the house. I need you to come get them."

"Be right there. I'm leaving now."

Then the fleet of U.S. government cars and two deputy sheriff's vehicles left the scene of the takedown, but not before what seemed like everyone I knew in the region drove by to see the circus.

CHAPTER 4

THE ARRAIGNMENT

"There is no more cruel tyranny than that which is exercised under cover of law, and with the colors of justice."

Baron Montesquieu, De L'Espirit Des Lois, 1748.

April 18 – 11 a.m. – Middle District to Western District

The familiar scenery to Charlotte changed inexplicably. Questions buzzed my mind.

Agent Curran used the term 'arraignment,' which meant there had been a grand jury hearing, though we set the appointment to come only days before. The Middle District of North Carolina, where we lived and owned property, would be the proper venue for any case against us. I would later learn from our New York attorney, the Middle District Office of the U.S. Attorney refused to be part of what it described as a "sham prosecution."

I was familiar with the process, having a law family and ex-wife as an attorney. A grand jury hearing was once an open affair where a neutral party presented facts to citizen-jurors in the pursuit of truth and justice. Today, however, these sessions are held in secret and a potential defendant or target is often not present and no one is allowed to have an attorney. This allows government a free hand for abuse.

The public prosecutor, an official position unknown to our Founding Fathers, can and frequently does lie or misrepresent situations at these hearings so as to get an indictment. The courts have determined, since the prosecutor is not under oath, he or she is not committing perjury.

I have worked on hundreds of such criminal cases during the past seven years and found it common practice for prosecutors to fabricate evidence and present staged witnesses reciting false testimony. I recently worked on a case where the agent openly lied to the grand jury for the prosecutor, under oath, while holding evidence proving what he said was perjured (*United States v. Charlie Engle,* Eastern District of Virginia). The court convicted Mr. Engle and has thus far refused to correct its error.

Prosecutors do these things with impunity due to a string of Supreme Court cases dating from 1967, *Pierson v. Ray,* which granted judges immunity. Within a year of the decision, prosecutors had the courts cover them as well. Prosecutors and federal judges are now immune from prosecution for crimes and misconduct, as long as they do it as part of what *they* consider to be their job. Unfortunately, there is almost no effective independent oversight of either judges or prosecutors. They are largely self-policing. Their considerable powers with little oversight allow them to work with few restraints.

A popular saying in first year law school is that a prosecutor today can "indict a ham sandwich." The more I thought about our situation en route to Charlotte, it was obvious the assistant U.S. Attorney in the Western District indicted two ham sandwiches, and we would be his lunch. I tried to figure out their strategy and decided they were most likely doing this so we could not return to The Bahamas, and to make us witnesses. They had to charge us with something in order to hold us.

What charges could they possibly have made up? Our firm paid handsomely each year for legal services to ensure we followed the law. I could not think of anything we did that could be used against us, yet here we were speeding to be arraigned in another jurisdiction's federal court.

Upon arrival in Charlotte, we were placed in the U.S. Marshal's holding cells in the federal courthouse, examined for tattoos and scars, photographed, and questioned thoroughly about everything from our bank accounts to personal habits.

The experience one hour later in the courtroom was more bizarre. Charges were read from an indictment including unrecognizable activities such as "conspiracy to defraud the United States," "obstruction of justice," "perjury," and "witness tampering," and then the duplication of the first charge, verbatim, to bulk up the indictment.

I never committed perjury or was a witness in a case to do so, nor did I know an indicted witness with whom to tamper. My wife was from Trinidad and our business was in The Bahamas. How and when were we supposed to have done these things?

After reading the charges very sternly, the judge asked me if I understood them, adding I faced up to forty-five years in prison. He did the same to my wife, and said she faced thirty-five years in prison.

We held each other's hands under the table. Even today, it is impossible for me to adequately describe my feelings at that moment. We were accused of things we had not done and knew nothing of, for which the judge said we could spend the rest of our lives in prison.

The two young attorneys for the government had rather smug expressions and were taking great pleasure in what they were doing. They knew the charges against us were false and contrived. In fact, the two had to have made up these stories for the grand jury.

"Do you understand the charges against you, Mr. Woltz?" the judge repeated, bringing me out of my ponderings.

"No sir. I don't understand any of this at all," I said.

Then it was over. The United States Government had arraigned us on false and unrecognizable charges, solely so we could be held and used as witnesses against someone else in matters of which we knew nothing. The agent in charge unabashedly confirmed this to me just days later. This could not be *my* America, the land I loved.

The indictment was frightening. *The United States vs. Howell Woltz and Vernice Woltz, Case No. 3:06-cr-074, United States District Court of North*

Carolina, Western District, Charlotte Division. Translation: the entire nation was against us.

An unstoppable avalanche began, one that would obliterate the lives we knew just hours before.

CHAPTER 5

THE FIRST NIGHT

"The function of the prosecutor under the Federal Constitution is not to tack as many skins of victims as possible to the wall. His function is to vindicate the right of people as expressed in the laws and give those accused of a crime a fair trial."

Donelly v. De Christofona, 416 US 637, 648-49, 40 L.Ed.2d. 431, 440, 94 S.Ct.1868 (1974)

April 18, 2006 – Mecklenburg County Jail, Charlotte, NC – Western District of North Carolina

After the arraignment I was put in a holding cell with several others and could not focus to read the thick Bill of Indictment. Men would leave the cell one at a time for their bond hearings, but none returned happy. Not one received bail.

I made a mental note to re-read the Constitution and see if perhaps I misunderstood the Eighth Amendment. The words certainly made clear its intention for defendants to get bail, adding the requirement that it not be "excessive."

After several hours, the court ran out of justice to dispense and called it quits for the day. My new companions and I were chained, handcuffed, and shackled for the short ride to the Mecklenburg County Jail, also in downtown Charlotte.

We shuffled our way into elevators and down steps in biting leg cuffs to be piled and packed into a small van. It was parked in the April sun in front of the loading dock of the courthouse. The temperature inside was at least one hundred and thirty degrees. The officer held me until last, which I greatly appreciated, and silently thanked him for the kindness.

Being singled out was not a favor. They rolled out our last companion in a wheelchair. He was a young man with shoulder-length dreadlocks. Due to a bullet in his spine put there by his brother, his bowels, bladder and legs were uncontrollable; the poor fellow soiled himself. The guards put me in and set him more on me than on the seat. The van door slammed shut.

We held him in place as best we could so he wouldn't fall to the floor. One of the men in the adjacent seat chocked him with his shoulder, and I held on to his sleeve, which was the only possible assistance I could give as my handcuffs were attached to a waist chain.

The chubby officer laughed, pointed and yelled, "Is it warm in there?" He went to the glassed-in front portion of the transportation van and made a show of fanning himself while enjoying the stream of air conditioning in his separate section.

The smell was overwhelming. Combined with the heat, it was all I could do not to throw up. Not one of these tough, street-wise guys said a word. The young man's obvious humiliation and the officer's intentional effort to demean us, left the van's individuals silent and forged.

As I saw my wife being led, walking in a slow shuffle to a waiting sedan, my own discomfort diverted. It was a defining moment. Vernice, partner and mother, was in sleepwear, chains and handcuffs. That picture indelibly imprinted itself on my brain.

Checking into the massive Mecklenburg County Jail was anything but a streamlined process. Its holding rooms were smaller, making our lengthy detention uncomfortable. Hardwood benches lined the walls with an open toilet in the corner. Every time the jailhouse guard came to take one of us to be finger-printed (again), photographed (again), and questioned (again), I asked when I would be allowed to see Doug, my waiting attorney.

Irritated by the unresponsiveness, I said it more forcefully and stood up while doing so.

"You'll see him when I'm damn well ready for you to see him! Are you threatening me?" asked the large officer in question.

"No, I'm not. But he's been waiting for me since nine-thirty this morning, and it's now seven p.m. He's just outside, sir," I said in my most polite tone of voice.

Forty-five minutes later the guard came to take me for the next round of torment, and I asked politely if he had any idea when I could see my attorney.

"He said he had to go; driving back to Raleigh or somewhere."

After another few hours, we were put on an elevator in small groups and taken up a few floors in the jail high-rise.

"Now we're getting somewhere," I said.

"Don't count on it, man," said one of my companions from the courthouse. "You're just getting started. The long wait is up here."

I assumed he was joking, as the *short* wait had already been five hours after waiting all afternoon in the holding cells at the courthouse.

He was not kidding. It was worse. The size of the rooms grew smaller. We were now down to closet-size, with nothing but a toilet and a bench that would hold two small men. None of the four of us was small.

We took turns on the tiny bench. The first fifteen minutes were mine because I sat down immediately upon entering. The large gentleman with tattoos on his neck took the next four hours and forty-five minutes. It worked out fine. He was sleepy, and I had some heavy thinking to do. I think best on my feet.

Eight or nine hours later, we were processed and ready to move on.

We were given ID bracelets and taken ten at a time to trade street clothes for the handsome, bright orange 'I'M GUILTY' suits I admired at the courthouse.

We were forced to shower in the presence of a guard, where we were told to lift our scrotum for inspection, bend over with spread buttocks cheeks and cough. Cavity, inguinal check and rinse-off complete, we donned our skimpy jailhouse attire, were given a two-inch toothbrush, a tiny tube of toothpaste just a bit larger than a tube of Super Glue, and a bar of soap.

The higher floors of the facility are comprised of *housing pods*. A pod is a double-deck enclosed unit with forty-eight to fifty-four cells, two TVs, a recreation area the size of a small living room and stainless steel dining tables with fixed metal stools attached to the concrete floor.

It was here we were given a sleeping mat, sheets, and a tiny towel. Those were my worldly possessions for the foreseeable future.

The jail guard was a chunky woman who looked perpetually angry. Her hair was pulled back so tightly it stretched the skin around her eyes. I asked her if she had pillows for us. She just stared at me. The other prisoners laughed, so I laughed too. I was a real hoot and didn't know it.

One of the men figured out by then I didn't have a clue, and told me quietly, "Roll up your pants and use them as a pillow."

It was after one a.m., and I'd done enough thinking on my feet for one day. The guard took me to a cell on the upper deck and slammed the large steel door, leaving a haunting echo reverberating through my body.

In an old prison movie some character said, "When a new batch first comes in, someone always cracks." I was hoping to not be that someone.

My eyes were killing me. The one-week disposable contact lenses were now four days old. I continued to wear a cheap pair of drug-store readers so they wouldn't be seized. Without both, I couldn't see my hands in front of my face. The contacts were +2.0; great for distance vision for driving, or to keep me from running into walls, and the readers were +2.0. Together, I had +4.0, which was necessary for me to see something up close.

I found a plastic pill cup left by a previous tenant, my new contact lens case, but had no contact solution. The previous guest in the 6' x 9' suite was something of a packrat and also left a package of salt, along with a few of sugar, mustard, and black pepper in the steel frame that was my bed.

I'd just finished making a saline solution for the contacts with the salt and put them in the pill cup when the lock of the steel door turned.

"Shakedown," the female guard said in a far less harsh tone than before. "Put your hands up against the door and spread your legs."

It was less than fifteen minutes since her last frisk. When the guard got to the groin area, she grabbed everything and whispered, "Looks like I got me a rich, white boy in my hands."

This was a new experience for me. "Yes, it looks as though you do," was the best response I could muster, not able to think of anything else to say to a lady jailer with a 50,000-volt Taser gun on her hip.

After the groping, the guard tore up the cot. She took the mustard, pepper, as well as my little lens cup, and threw the liquid into the toilet bowl, contacts and all, just as I was saying, "Don't! Those are my contact lenses."

"Oh. Too bad," she said, putting the empty cup on the steel shelf above the toilet and slammed the steel door with a resounding clang.

I sank to the floor by the toilet and put my head at its rim. "Please, God. I'm sure all of this is for some purpose, but don't leave me where I can't see. Please."

Sitting on the floor of a nasty jail cell with my head on a prison toilet, praying to see was a rather low moment. As I wheeled and dealt with the Great Creator over my eyesight, the dead silence of the cell block was broken by a scream, followed by wailing from below.

"Let me out! I don't belong here! Please! Let me out." The moans and cries eventually turned to whimpers and then silence.

I lay there against the toilet with my eyes closed, vacillating between self-pity and appreciation. I hadn't been the first to crack. No tears were shed, and I had not broken. I promised that moment these people would never elicit either response no matter how long this nightmare lasted.

When my eyes opened seconds later, there were blurs, drops of the homemade saline solution on the toilet seat, including a large, perfectly round one, reflecting in the light. I put on the reading glasses and squinted.

When I touched the big drop, it stuck to my finger. I immediately put the single contact in and searched the floor, toilet, and even the bowl for the other to no avail.

One would do. I begged the heavens to let me see, but I didn't say with how many eyes. I should have been more specific. My prayer was answered, nonetheless.

At that moment, a certain indescribable peace came over me. I knew I would survive this, no matter what they threw at me. There was a reason all this was happening, I thought. I needed to begin looking for it.

It was freezing in the tiny cell. The short-sleeved jail outfit was like a pair of pajamas. I balled up the pants for a pillow, and lay down on the mat atop the steel plate, covered myself with the thin blanket and fell into a deep sleep. It was chilly without pants, but they did make a good pillow. The old boy who told me the new trick understood what he was talking about.

CHAPTER 6

THE INFAMOUS MECKLENBURG COUNTY JAIL

"If the government, police and prosecutors could always be trusted to do the right thing, there would have never been a need for the Bill of Rights."

Ninth Circuit Justice Leventhal, United States v. U.S. District Court for the Central District of California, 858 F.2d. 534 (9th Circuit, 1988)

April 19, 2006 4:15 a.m. – Western District of North Carolina

S leep was deep but short. A strange popping noise began at some distance, came closer and louder. There was a hiss. The door popped open; its air lock released. The unfamiliar noises were disorienting, but once awake, the strangeness continued.

The guard screamed for everyone to get down stairs for roll call. I tried to block out her voice in hopes of slipping back into the comfort of sleep, but she would have none of it, going from cell to cell, screaming insults and orders.

My pillow reverted to elastic-waist orange prison pants. "Salt," I told myself. "Salt to make contact lens solution, remember to find salt."

My brain was beginning to function.

The female guard lined us in alphabetical order and called the roll as if we were in kindergarten, except with an angry voice. She went straight through the roll again, only now handing out heavy, molded plastic trays with skimpy portions of grits, powdered eggs, and two slices of white bread.

I sat down at one of the nine steel hexagon tables and stared at the tray.

An older homeless-looking man across the table watched and said, "Hey man, ain't you hungry?"

I shook my head and slid the tray across the table to him.

"I'm not going to be in here long enough to get hungry for crap like this."

One of the men seated at the table, in kind voice but gentler demeanor than I deserved, said, "Man, you best eat. You're in Mecklenburg County now with a Fed bracelet on. You ain't going nowhere but prison from here."

I hoped he was wrong, but his tone was very sincere.

The Eighth Amendment guarantees the right to bail. From my history studies, I knew there wasn't a jail in the United States to hold a "pre-trial detainee," as we were called, when the amendment was written in 1789, so everyone must have gotten bail in our nation's early years. Pennsylvania Quakers opened the first jail in post-revolutionary America in 1790, *after* the States approved the Eighth Amendment. The Walnut Street Jail, as it was known, never held a "pre-trial detainee," only those convicted by a jury.

While hoping this fellow was wrong, I feared he was not from what I witnessed the prior day. Breakfast ended and the angry guard ordered us back to our cells. I forgot the salt to make lens solution. It was only 4:45 a.m. No sooner had I re-entered the subconscious did I hear the popping sounds followed by the raised voice of the guard. "Shift change! Shift change! Get down stairs now for shift change!"

As the men slowly assembled, the guard uttered continuous assaults. "Shirts tucked into your pants, and get your hands out of them! I don't want to see no asses hanging out of them neither! Anybody that ain't down here in line in two minutes is locked down for the day!"

The clock on the wall read 6:30 a.m.

Someone in line said, "Man down," a call announcing the replacement guard was at the entrance, known as the *slider*. Everyone was deathly quiet.

The heavy glass and steel doors opened and in walked the day-shift guard. The two swapped a few words and laughed, but when they were done, the same angry look took over the day guard's face, and she called the roll, yet again.

We were instructed to file by, show our armband and take a seat at a table for orientation. After her lengthy speech, and for the second time in less than three hours, we were locked down.

The Charlotte-Mecklenburg County Jail, like many prisons, uses sleep deprivation to keep prisoners docile. Schedules are designed to make it impossible to sleep for more than four continuous hours. Sleep deprivation and disruption are powerful tools. This reminded me of the time when our children were infants, our getting up and down, feeding and changing diapers at all hours. We constantly craved sleep. What I would have given at this moment, however, to hear their young cries and attend them.

By nine a.m., it was "up" again. The jailhouse outfit was thin poplin. We were nearly naked, and I was freezing. The guard announced we could not use our blankets until night or be caught lying on our beds, under penalty of punishment.

We played alphabetical line-up again at eleven o'clock to get our lunch, which I also gave away. We were locked down again for a few hours, "up" again at two o'clock, then another alphabetical line-up at four o'clock for dinner, "down" again after that, then "up" again for another alphabetical line-up for yet another shift change and orientation speech at seven o'clock, then another lock down, then up again until we were locked in our cells for the night.

I wondered if my wife was having the same treatment in the women's pod. Had she been able to contact anyone? Did Kate, Chris and John know what happened to us? Would they think of us as criminals? I could not bear the thought of our children thinking of us in that way. How could I communicate we had done no wrong when the most powerful government in the world said otherwise?

Had we committed a crime, I would have admitted it to them and gone on, but nothing for which we were charged had basis in truth. Our trust company was small but meticulous. Attorney Hiram Martin, formerly of Gibson Dunn & Crutcher, designed our structures and trust deeds. He crafted the same structure for President Reagan. There was nothing cutting edge about our work, nor was it in any grey area of law. Hiram personally signed the trust deeds for our few American clients, certifying they were in compliance with U.S. law. By 2006, this former presidential trust attorney was a member of our board as well as a partner.

"What was this really about?" I wondered. It certainly wasn't about something we had done. The charges were unrecognizable.

CHAPTER 7

BOND HEARING – PART 1

"Fourth Amendment was drafted to quell pretrial deprivation of liberty." Torres v. McLaughlin, 163 F.3d. 169 (3rd Cir. 1998)

April 20, 2006 3:45 a.m. – Western District of North Carolina

Paper is sold in jail and I had none, so I used the back of the indictment to write a line-by-line refutation of the charges against us until the early morning hours. When the cell door opened there was no popping sound or screaming guard, just a voice from the speaker.

"Woltz, you got court this morning."

"Night court?" I wondered as I fumbled for reading glasses, hoping to first see the cup with contact lens. The salty solution had brined its contents and burned my left eye. Momentarily, one lens was better than two.

Contact in and tears subsiding, I saw the clock downstairs, 3:45 a.m.

"Woltz! Hurry it up. Don't want to keep the judge waiting," came over the speaker.

"Yes, dear," I said sarcastically, but quietly, I thought.

"What was that, Woltz? I don't need any lip off you this morning. You got two minutes to get your ass in that slider."

Disheveled and in need of coffee, I piled out of the cell sporting bright orange wear and thong flip-flops.

At the guard's workstation, I asked, "Where do I change into my clothes for court, here or at the courthouse?"

She looked as if I were from another planet, which is exactly how I felt. "You're in your court clothes far as I know."

"I can't go into court looking like this! I look like a criminal in this thing!"

"Well you ain't in here for your good looks, Woltz. Must have done something. But that ain't my problem. Getting your butt in that slider over there is."

She pointed where several others waited. The enclosure has two sets of doors, one to the cell block, and one to the jail hallway. After a twenty-minute wait, a guard appeared at the outer door, and slid his ID card down the electronic key-gate.

"Follow me, single-file, right-hand side of the hallway." One set of instructions and off we moved toward the elevator.

Once downstairs, we packed into the *bullpen,* a holding cell already full of men.

An hour passed, the door opened and men who appeared lifeless shot up and moved toward it. I happened to be near the entrance. The guard moved, dispensing paper sacks.

"Hold the bottom. It's wet," he instructed.

I grabbed one. Other men circled back for a second. In jail, he who hesitates goes hungry. Those in the back of the line shouted when the bags ran out.

He held up his empty hands and said, "I had one for each of you. If you can't get it, that's your problem."

I was starving by day three. There were four slices of white bread, compacted as one and a slimy, plastic baggie with two slices of mystery meat and yellow squares, the makings of cheese. The meal was made complete by a drink of sugar juice and an orange. I traded the sandwiches and drink for oranges.

When the door opened and the guard came to pick up the breakfast trash, I tried again to get my clothes.

"When do we change for court? I have a bond hearing this morning and need to get dressed." He just looked at me, shook his head, and said, "You're pretty funny, man," and left.

"You're in your court clothes," said another prisoner. "It takes a court order to get these guys to let you wear your own, and that's not happening in Charlotte, North Carolina. These guys want you looking as guilty as possible every time you come into the courtroom."

"That can't be legal," I said, indignantly.

"Man, this is Charlotte, the most corrupt federal jurisdiction in the United States. The law is the last thing these cats worry about."

I stared through the window down the hallway looking to evaluate the place and time. Eight a.m. We'd waited four hours and hadn't left the jail.

"Don't want to keep the judge waiting," the upstairs guard said.

Who does the waiting in their world was an interesting concept.

It was inconceivable to me courts and prosecutors were allowed to force un-convicted citizens to wear bright orange jail uniforms into court before they were found guilty. It couldn't help but prejudice all who saw them, including the judge. You could dress up the Pope in one of these outfits, and he'd be found guilty as well.

While still processing the thought I'd be attending federal court in bright orange pajamas, the U.S. marshals arrived with their leather tool bags full of chains and cuffs. My attire was about to get worse.

They brought my wife out of the women's holding cell. She looked as if she had cried all night. I watched them put a long chain around her waist, leg chains and shackles on her bare ankles, and hook handcuffs through the stout waist-chain. She was a fixture. Her face, a mixture of defiance, sadness and humility, reinforced my anger for what these people were doing.

I caught her eye, and we stared at one another through the glass. There were no words. The whole situation was surreal.

We boarded the transport to the federal courthouse, were brought through the rear of the building, and placed in the same holding cells from two days ago. I was unable to speak with Vernice. They told us to stay apart and when I tried to approach her, the guards yelled.

After an hour, a marshal came to the cell. "Woltz?"

I was taken to the same room where the interrogation had occurred the day of arrest. A somewhat familiar face was on the other side of the heavy glass. He pointed to a phone on the wall.

"Howell? I'm David Freedman, an attorney with Fred Crumpler's office in Winston-Salem. Laurie called and asked me to be here today."

Laurie is my ex-wife, a lawyer now judge. Fred Crumpler was my hunting buddy for years. "I thought you looked familiar," I said. "I've seen you at Fred's office."

"Right, I thought you might recognize me. We only have a minute, so I'll tell you about myself. I was recently named the best criminal defense attorney in North Carolina by the State Bar Magazine." He held up a magazine with his picture on the front cover, his hand obscuring the title.

"Laurie suggested your family retain me. Do you have any problem with that?"

"None whatsoever. I'm just glad to have somebody come and get me out of here."

"That's what this morning is all about. How did you plead, guilty or not guilty?" His comment threw me. I pled *not guilty* at the arraignment. Freedman did not appear to be familiar with the case, what little had happened. How much file was necessary to read?

"We didn't do anything!" I replied. "I don't understand why we're in here! I'm mailing you the indictment with my notes on it, today, to prove it."

"Well they certainly seem to think you did something, but we'll deal with that later. Are you sure you want to plead 'not guilty'?"

Now I was concerned. My attorney was suggesting I plead guilty and hadn't asked a single question about the case.

"Damn right. I'm telling you this is nonsense. I don't know what they are talking about!"

Freedman gave me one of those 'that's what they all say' looks. Our discussion and preparation for the bond hearing were apparently over. He stood up and said, "I'll see you out there in just a few minutes." The finality of our brief encounter was punctuated by his hanging up the phone and efficient departure.

I was in disbelief. What had just happened? The receiver dangled in my hand.

The return to holding was brief. I was chained to the teeth, and we were taken to the courtroom.

As we entered, I saw my dear mother, my brothers, my ex-wife, our friend, Robert Cook, and a handful of other associates and relatives.

I had not spoken by phone to anyone since Agent Curran allowed the phone call to Robert to pick up the boys, and yet there they were for us.

We were unchained in front of the judge, but this did not diminish our appearance as criminals in jail uniforms. The chains were just icing on the cake.

My mother blinked back tears as she watched the orchestrated spectacle. Our eyes locked, and she mouthed, "I love you," from the gallery, aside brothers Jim and Thomas.

The show began.

First up was a young prosecutor who looked to be twenty-five. He introduced himself as Assistant U.S. Attorney Kurt Meyers and said he represented the United States of America against us.

He began by waving a sheaf of paper, claiming my wife and I had extensive criminal records.

"Whoa!" I blurted, coming out of the chair, "We don't have *any* criminal record!"

"The best criminal defense lawyer in North Carolina" let that pass. Freedman pulled me down and told me not to do that again.

"But he's lying!" I said, loud enough for the judge to hear.

The Honorable Judge David Keesler hearing this, ordered AUSA Meyers to turn over the pages to read for himself. My wife had no record of convictions, and mine consisted of a citation for speeding at the age of seventeen. The rest of the pages were blank.

"Come on guys. Speeding reduced to improper equipment?" said Judge Keesler in disbelief. The judge caught the prosecutor's sham and lie, but AUSA Meyers didn't seem to be embarrassed.

The theatrics continued. He told the judge we were *conspirators* of international note, but included no details. Our owning of foreign financial firms was equated with criminal activity. He claimed we had accounts in Bermuda and Switzerland, and could get there in our jet to retrieve the money. These contentions were also lies.

He then told the judge I would go to the airport and steal a plane if he let us go. Which was it? Did I have my own jet or would I steal one?

I hadn't owned or been licensed to fly a plane in fifteen years, but it didn't stop the boys from the U.S. Attorney's Office from claiming otherwise.

Meyers untruthfully claimed we had permanent residency in The Bahamas, and would flee there if let go. I was on a student visa as a doctoral candidate in Nassau; Vernice and John were on temporary visas and had to leave every ninety days.

Residency is a legal status, like someone in the U.S. having a green card. It is also a status I've never enjoyed in The Bahamas, and these assistant U.S. attorneys knew it. They were trying to paint us as a *flight risk* to prevent our release on bond.

Meyers's closing went along these lines: When I stole a plane (since I used to be a pilot long ago), and flew us to our place of 'residence' (where we couldn't stay because we weren't 'residents'), we could not be extradited, because there was no extradition treaty with The Bahamas. Not a word of it was true or believable, including the issue of extradition. The Bahamas' Extradition Treaty with the United States was one of the first acts of Parliament after the new nation became independent of Great Britain in the 1970's.

Having no reason to hold us, the U.S. attorney's office decided to make up one. Fortunately, they lied so boldly and with such audacity Judge Keesler didn't buy it either.

I imagined what these prosecutors told the grand jury to get the indictment. If they would lie this openly to a Federal Magistrate Judge in our presence, how far did they go in their *secret* grand jury room?

With each concocted lie, I nudged Attorney Freedman.

"That's a lie! Say something!"

"Shh! Not now," he kept responding.

For the *coup de grace*, AUSA Meyers turned and fired his eye on us while pointing his finger. "The defendants are a threat to the community! These are DAAANNNGGGEERROUS PEOPLE!!!"

Vernice looked at me quizzically, as if to say, "Is he talking about us?" We were the only people in the courtroom wearing jail suits and leg shackles, so it seemed obvious.

But that wasn't enough for the young prosecutor. He ended by claiming I was "an economic threat to the United States of America!"

The United States economy quivers at the mention of my name, according to this imaginative man. He told the judge I was so powerful I had an enormously wealthy "Watchdog" who would "sweep out of the sky and whisk me away to a safe haven, even if it took a million dollars."

Throughout all of this, "the best criminal defense attorney in North Carolina" sat glued to his seat and speechless. Freedman slouched like he was taking a nap.

The prosecutor's aggressiveness, as nonsensical as it was, stunned me. It seemed to convey something bigger. It didn't, however, surprise Judge Keesler. He moved side to side while announcing, "That story is bizarre."

He then ordered us released on unsecured bond.

Before I could finish hugging my wife in celebration, Meyers raised his arm and screamed, "Government appeals, Your Honor." Marshals descended in seconds, putting us in chains. We were not going to be freed after all.

My mother came up to the railing and said, "I still love you."

"You didn't believe any of that, did you Momma?" I mouthed or thought. I don't know which.

As they dragged us away, I looked over my shoulder and saw my flesh and blood staring back. In their faces I saw sadness but also shock, shame, sorrow, and resignation that I must be a crook. My heart broke then and there.

Yep. We only thought we knew old Howell for the last half-century. It must have been the speeding ticket back in 1970 that started him on a life of crime.

One doesn't imagine being in these situations before they occur. There is no preparation for such events. Vernice and I couldn't muster a word. We waddled, chained, to our holding cells.

CHAPTER 8

FIRST WEEKEND IN JAIL

"Bail Reform Act requires release of person facing trial under least restrictive condition or combination of conditions that will reasonably assure appearance of person as required and safety of community; only in rare circumstances should release be denied, and doubts regarding propriety of release should be resolved in defendant's favor."

United States v. Gebro, 948 F.2d. 1118 (9th Cir. 1991)

April 21, 2006 – Western District of North Carolina

The Bail Reform Act's only "reform" has been to eliminate bond for all but a few defendants. We were extremely lucky to be granted bond by Judge Keesler, but I had no idea what would happen next. My attorney did not waste any time coming back into Marshal's holding to tell me. Depression accompanied me back to the pod.

I had no phone access because the PIN code I was given by the jailers did not work. According to my new friends and advisors, that was standard operating procedure when one was a *guest of the Feds*, as they called them.

"They play dirty, man," one of them said. "Feds don't want you talking to nobody, unless you are working for them."

It was the weekend, and the pod was void of reading material except Seventh Day Adventist and Nation of Islam tracts.

Much of my faith developed along Native American traditions, where The Creator was found in nature or one's own heart. I was intrigued with the simplicity of this oldest of ways. There are no rules or laws except to respect others and all creation. Respect includes appreciation of all paths to the divine as well, thereby eliminating inter-religion squabbles, the fuel for most wars today. I was learning the ways prior to prison. If all life came from what was once a molten rock flying through dark space, then we must all be related. This original American religion existed thousands of years before the European invasion. Every tree, flower, animal, and fish, I was told by an Elder, was not something to be used and abused, but a brother or sister of Creation. Each must be treated with respect. Each held the divine spark, which was in that stone heart of the planet when it cooled, and from which all life sprang. That divine spark was our Father, and the earth was our Mother. Both were to be cherished, as were all other forms and features of the world.

Nature was my temple, and I was lost in a concrete high-rise, where nothing of it could be seen. I walked circles imagining myself in the woods at the farm. The cheap flip-flops ate at my feet. I tried to meditate, but worried about the children too much to enter that tranquil world. I had no means of contacting family or my friend, the Chief of Police, who was keeping the boys, so I went back to the recreation yard and walked barefoot.

I sold my dinner tray for stamps and an envelope and sent the refutation I'd written on the back of the indictment to David Freedman in the evening mail. With that information, even if he was the *worst* attorney in the state rather than the "best" as he claimed, we could beat the made-up charges.

After the second hour of walking in circles a nice man in his late twenties opened up a conversation. He was doing inverted push-ups, standing on his hands with his feet high on the wall. He was doing lots of them. I marveled. I'd never seen this before.

His name was Eugene, and he led me gently into a conversation of brutal honesty and accuracy of what lay ahead. It was the first time my fate and situation were clear.

"What are you doing in here?" he asked. "You don't exactly look like you belong."

Eugene's speech was as straight forward as his message. He wore small eyeglasses that gave him a distinctive, professorial look.

"I don't know," I answered as honestly as I could. "I really don't."

"If that's true, which I don't doubt, then they want something from you," he said casually, between rounds of being upside down. "They must want you to testify against somebody else. They've got you in here to squeeze you so you'll do what they tell you to do."

Not ready to spill my guts to a stranger, I shifted the conversation. "How about you? How long have you been here?"

"Nine months."

"Nine months!" I shouted. "You've been waiting in here for nine months? They can't do that!"

Eugene laughed softly, and said, "Many others have been here much longer than I have. You'll realize pretty soon they do anything they want these days. These people don't follow any rules. You either do what they want you to do, or you sit in jail until you've had all you can stand.

"There's an old man from the Dominican Republic they've held here for several years," Eugene continued. "He won't say what they want him to say, but they can't take him to trial because they don't have any evidence against him."

In my naiveté, I asked, "Then why don't they just let him go and admit they made a mistake?"

Eugene broke into a pleasant smile and said, "You really are new to all this, aren't you?"

"Yes. I guess I am."

"If they let him go after all of this time, he could sue them for false imprisonment, so they've got to wear him down now until he agrees to plead guilty to something, anything really, so they can justify holding him. They will *never* admit to a mistake," Eugene concluded.

"That's so insidious," was all I could muster in response.

"I've been in here for nine months because I won't plead guilty to something I didn't do and won't lie on the stand for them about people I don't know and things I never saw or knew about. Just trying to wait them out now," he said.

"What could they possibly want from me? I work in the financial industry down in The Bahamas."

Eugene smiled again, "You can bet they want you to say something about somebody you know or you wouldn't be in here."

"They've got my wife in here too," I said, opening up to this stranger more than I intended to.

"Then they really want you to say something and figure they need some leverage. That's pretty common these days. They grab somebody you love and put the pressure on that way. Then they can make you say anything they want, true or not. It works."

"How do they get away with it?"

"No one cares what they do to people in here unless they've been in here and experienced it themselves. Let me ask you. Before a few days ago, did you give a darn whether they treated people in jail fairly or not, or care even a bit about what happened to folks accused of a crime?"

He answered his own question before I could, "Of course not. My guess is you were a 'Get-tough-on-crime,' hard-core Republican until about three days ago," which stung, because it was pretty close to the mark except that I was an independent.

"Whether the cops and prosecutors followed the law, or respected the rights of defendants, was the last thing on your mind, because you never thought you'd be one of us. Am I close?"

My silence confirmed it. The young man just read me like a book.

"But my wife?"

"My guess is they want you to lie if they've got her in here. If all they wanted you to do were tell the truth, then they wouldn't need her for leverage. Having you would be enough. They do that to make sure they get what they want. Who are your co-defendants?"

"One is an attorney down in Wilmington who sent us a couple of clients. I hardly know him. The other is a former U.S. Attorney and judge from Raleigh," I answered. "He was also head of the Republican Party for several years."

Eugene chuckled. "You've got a U.S. Attorney, who was also a judge and politico, and you're wondering what they want with you? Man, he's a trophy to these people. I hate to tell you this, but they'll do anything in the world to keep you on ice until they need you. It makes sense now."

I really didn't like hearing this, but it did make sense in a perverse sort of way.

"I'm beginning to think that too, after talking to you. We got bond, unsecured, in fact, from Judge Keesler yesterday, but the prosecutors appealed it. I didn't even know they could do that."

"They do anything they want these days. I'm surprised Keesler gave you bond. Even the judges are scared of these prosecutors. If they appealed it, then you can bet they're out looking for the right judge now, so they can hold you," he said, "but they've got to appeal to a judge in this district, and Judge Mullen is fair."

"They can't pick the judge," I said. "That would be judge-shopping. It's against the law."

Eugene's stare made complete our understanding. I was ignorant and naïve. It was too depressing on a variety of levels, and I didn't want to talk about it anymore.

"How did you get those combat boots?" I asked. "Everyone else has flip flops or sneakers."

"I clean the place. Medical gave me a shoe pass."

"Can I help you today? I've got to have something to do or I'm going to go crazy in here," wishing I'd left off the last part of the sentence.

We spent the next few hours scrubbing showers, sweeping, mopping, and cleaning the whole place. I enjoyed the work, being out of the solitary cell, and talking to this very bright companion.

His passion was art. As he informally exhibited his work after dinner, a crowd gathered. One of the men at the table was upset. He explained it was his son's birthday, and his gift needed to be a card, one proudly depicting the son's favorite cartoon character.

Eugene agreed to make one, but the child was a fan of Sponge Bob Square Pants. Neither the father nor Eugene had any idea what he looked like. Sponge Bob was new at the time.

The man was distraught. His promise and the child's request would not be met. I moved a table away, observing, touched by the scene. Seven men were huddled together trying to work out what to do about a child's birthday card. He wasn't their child, but they could appreciate the man's emotional turmoil. Eugene drew a few other characters, but they weren't Sponge Bob Square Pants. Only one had ever seen the cartoon, and he couldn't adequately describe Sponge Bob's appearance in enough detail for Eugene to draw him.

The father became so distraught I really thought he would cry. The others around the table were tough-looking, street-wise men, but their compassion and understanding were on display.

While the father and his advisors lamented, Eugene sketched. Just when everyone was about to give up, Eugene slid a drawing over to the father and tapped him on the shoulder.

He saw the offering, gave a big grin and said, "Pooh Bear!" as everyone *oohed* and *aahed* over Eugene's work.

"Every kid likes Pooh Bear," said one.

Eugene captured the essence of the world's best-loved bruin to the T, walking with balloon in hand and honey pot clutched to his chest.

"Pooh-Bear has always been his favorite. He'll like that just fine, Eugene," the father said.

The crisis was over, but tasks remained for the artist and me. Eugene completed the card while I worked to absorb the meaning of the event.

These tough men were outwardly menacing, intent on threatening others. I assumed the vicious and mean appearances were their nature. That was my prejudice. I would never have known them as otherwise were it not for today. It dawned on me their actions and demeanor were necessary survival skills, a hostile response to a hostile place, *the street*, a world I knew nothing about. I witnessed a tender moment where the real nature of these fellows shone through. I was taught an invaluable lesson and would never see them in the same way again.

My thoughts returned to the artist after the others left.

"You've got talent, Eugene," I said, needing to make conversation.

"I hope to get some formal training when I get out of here, and maybe go into commercial art."

"When I get out, would you like for me to send some art books?"

He looked up from his work. "*If* you get out. Sorry to be negative, but it sounds like we're in the same boat. If they have your wife in here as a hostage, you may be in worse shape than me. You might be in here a long time while they try to break you down. The sooner you start getting your mind wrapped around the thought, the better off you'll be."

That was the first time it occurred to me I might actually be stuck in jail for years like those who wouldn't plead guilty or lie.

"You need to find something you can do to keep your mind busy. What do you like to do?"

"Not much I can do in this place," I responded.

"Start drawing. It'll keep your mind off of what's happening to you and your wife."

"That child would cry if he saw my Pooh Bear, Eugene."

"Well, you need to think of something, unless you want to waste your time in front of the TV like most of these guys do."

The reality of my situation was coming clear, and it was not good. My dwindling confidence was being replaced by a growing sickness. It was not exactly nausea, but rather a horrible sense of foreboding. Our lives were slipping away. Powerful and seemingly unstoppable forces were at work.

I needed some solace. This was all getting bigger than I could handle, and my young friend was right. I needed to find something to hang on to. I needed something to focus on, to keep my sanity in an insane situation.

Meditation had been a part of my routine since spending time in India in the 1990s, and I decided to seek its solace. It was also time to start looking for the meaning in all of this. There had to be one. I needed to figure out how to survive and not just physically. It was a tough place, no doubt, and more than a bit disconcerting to be one of the only white guys and the most senior. I'd lived through nine coups and revolutions in Haiti, endured some things none of these men would believe. Plus, with a new perspective on my fellow prisoners, unless I did something stupid or let things spin out of control, I would be OK. The challenge would be to muster mental toughness. Even the most hardened guys dealt with that too.

Scrubbing and mopping served two purposes. The nasty condition of the facility greatly improved, and I was worn out physically. I knew the mind and body would soon rest, if I could also stop thinking about Eugene's words.

What if I *were* stuck in here? What could I do with my time that would be productive?

I washed out the dirty prison uniform in the shower, along with the boxer shorts I'd worn since being abducted days before. These were the only clothes I had, so I put them back on in the shower, wet and returned to my cell.

It was freezing. I spread out the clothes as best I could in the tiny space in hopes they would dry by four a.m. and got under the thin blanket, naked and cold, hoping to get warm enough to sleep. I said a little prayer asking for guidance and direction.

It didn't take long to get my initial answer. I decided to make notes each day and keep a journal of events. I would tell this story.

CHAPTER 9

ROAD TRIP WITH THE U.S. MARSHALS

Rule 18, Federal Rules of Criminal Procedure

"The government must prosecute an offense in a district where the offense was committed."

18 U.S.C. § 3232- District of offense

"Proceedings to be in district and division in which offense committed."

Jurisdiction-legal definition

"Under federal law and court rules, a court may exercise its inherent authority only if it has two types of jurisdiction: personal and subject matter. Personal Jurisdiction is the authority that a court has over the parties in the case. Subject Matter Jurisdiction is a court's authority over the particular claim or controversy. Jurisdiction is the power and authority constitutionally conferred upon a court or judge to pronounce the sentence of law over a certain area or certain persons of a particular geographic area containing a defined legal authority." The Law Dictionary

April 23, 2006 – Three federal jurisdictions in one day—Western, Middle and Eastern Districts of North Carolina

Four a.m. rolled around once again, and the ridiculous ritual of line up and scream replayed itself for another day. Oatmeal gruel and a single, tiny waffle square replaced the usual powdered eggs and grits. It was the Sunday special. Other than minor changes in the starvation diet, one day was already becoming indiscernible from another.

My routine was falling into place, just in time to be disrupted. Morning meditation was completed during lock down after breakfast. I replaced the hour formerly occupied with self-pity, by walking briskly in a circle on the tiny recreation yard, while imagining I was out in nature. I'd walked long enough that morning for the uniform to dry out from the night before, when one of the guards yelled.

"Woltz! Pack your shit and get your ass in the slider. You got five minutes. Marshals are waiting downstairs. Don't make 'em come up and get you."

Somebody was always waiting, but I never knew why.

I did not have a clue what was being done to us. It was a Sunday, so it could not be court-related, and my lawyer had not made any contact or advised of any hearing. I was hopeful they realized it was all a mistake. Maybe David Freedman really was the best attorney and was working behind the scenes. Perhaps the nightmare was over.

It didn't take long to pack. All I had were the skimpy jail clothes I wore and my notes made on paper Eugene had given me. I was packed and ready to leave in two minutes. The guard said five, so I had three to spare. The U.S. marshals were apparently not in too big a hurry. They left me in the slider for nearly a half hour before someone finally came to escort me downstairs. Once on the ground floor, I was put in a holding cell, alone.

Shortly thereafter, I saw my wife pass by with a guard and caught her eye. She shrugged her shoulders as if to say, I don't know what's happening either. They put her nearby. In a surprisingly short amount of "Fed time," we were hustled out of the holding cells, told to get out of our jail pajamas, and given our street clothes.

They were wadded up in plastic sacks. We changed and exited in our wrinkled garb, exchanging glances cautiously, still trying to figure out what was going on. Were we being released? Were the marshals taking us home?

An older gentleman with grey hair entered. He wore a fishing vest over a knit shirt and khaki pants. A short, dark-haired woman trailed him. Everyone seemed to know the man and like him.

He was U.S. marshal Jimmy Spivey. He was very polite to my wife, which was refreshing.

Marshal Spivey chained and trussed us while telling us we were not to sit together or speak to one another. That answered one question. The marshals were not here to take us home. He put us in the van, one in front of the other. With his C.C. Rider tape blaring in front, I was able to put my head against the back of Vernice's and speak to her without being noticed or heard.

I asked if she knew why or where we were being taken, or who was behind it. She knew no more than I. There were a hundred things I wanted to say and ask, but all I could do at that moment was put my head to the back of hers and enjoy a moment of contact.

We rode the highway out of Charlotte more or less in silence. We had no idea where they were taking us or why. I knew the Sixth Amendment required any adjudication of our case to occur within the district of charge, which was where they claimed a crime had been committed. Jurisdiction is the power of a court to exercise its legal authority, and under Article III, §2, as well as the Sixth Amendment, that power only existed in the Charlotte Division of the Western Judicial District of North Carolina, once the charges were brought there.

Once jurisdiction attaches, rightly or wrongly, only that court can hear or decide that case for its duration. Jurisdiction becomes exclusive at that point.

Venue is another important legal concept. It is the geographical region where the authority of the court of jurisdiction can be exercised, and venue attaches after jurisdiction. Under Venue Rule 18 of the Federal Rules of Criminal Procedure, venue in our case was the Charlotte Division of the Western District of North Carolina, and we could not (legally) be taken from it for any reason.

The Founding Fathers added this protection to prevent citizens from being dragged from their home, out of sight and mind, to a jurisdiction where improper things could be done. The British were known to have done this before the American Revolution and our Constitution forbids it.

We never did business in the Western District or lived there, but once jurisdiction *attached* in that district and division, even though improper, it was set as a matter of decided law. Fighting it beyond that point would have been a waste of time. But taking us out of that *jurisdiction* and *venue*, once both attached, was a federal crime under 18 U.S.C. §3232 , which states, "Proceedings to be in district and division in which offense committed." Moving us from Charlotte, even to another Western District Court, would be a violation of federal law as well as Rule 18 of the Federal Rules of Criminal Procedure and the Sixth Amendment, though I did not know it at the time. That was my attorney's job, had he chosen to do it.

When Marshal Spivey turned onto I-40 headed for Raleigh, I knew something was very wrong, I just did not know how many federal laws were being broken. We were not only being hijacked from the Charlotte Division, we were on our way out of the Western District altogether. Three and a half hours and two federal jurisdictions later, we pulled into the underground garage of the Wake County Jail in downtown Raleigh, in the Eastern District of North Carolina.

The prosecutors from Charlotte took no chances. What they did was immoral, unethical, and a federal crime. We were not only in a foreign district without any Constitutional authority to rule in our case, we were apparently going to the same court where their target, Sam Currin, had been the U.S. Attorney. Eastern North Carolina was a Democratic stronghold since the founding of the party back in the 1800s. Sam Currin had not only been a Republican prosecutor there, but State Chairman of the Republican Party as well. He had very few friends in Democratic Eastern North Carolina. Taking us there was illegal and diabolically brilliant.

Martens, Meyers, and whatever judge allowed this illegal move, put us in a no-win situation. We were far from home and jurisdiction, in a hostile environment for any case involving Sam Currin. AUSA Meyers painted us as Sam Currin's close associates at the hearing in Charlotte, which I did not understand at the time.

It was our firm that forced Sam Currin to move his business. As Chairman of Sterling Trust, I personally filed the suspicious activity report, which likely, but inadvertently, started the whole case when the Central Bank of The Bahamas shared it with the U.S. government. That made AUSA Meyers' assertion of our close ties to Currin all the more strange, but I was beginning to understand what he did and why. Had they planned this as a back-up strategy in case we were granted bond by the court of jurisdiction?

Mr. Spivey and the female marshal un-cuffed, un-trussed, and placed us in the custody and care of The Wake County Jail. In ritualized form, we were put into separate holding cells for a long time and then stripped once more of our street clothes and dignity. I did the scrotum show, spread buttocks, and coughed for Officer Ramos so he could make sure the U.S. marshals hadn't given me some contraband to carry.

The only thought more repulsive than the idea of transporting something in such a manner is the notion of using it. I was issued a V-neck top with elastic-waist pants sporting six-inch alternating bright orange and white horizontal stripes from top to bottom. It was also three sizes too big, and there was a no-exchange policy. It hurt to look at it.

A couple of hours later, we were both taken to see a nurse who asked us more personal and invasive questions. There was no one else waiting in the early afternoon, so we zipped through in a record four or five hours, half the usual time.

We were re-chained, though already in the secure portion of the jail, and rode the elevator to our separate accommodations. When my guard and I arrived on the fifth floor, I was unchained and ordered to grab a mat from a filthy room that was once used for prisoner exercise.

The recreation area became storage for sleeping mats and recycled plastic sacks, though still very much the law that exercise must be allowed prisoners daily. Each sack contained soap, toothbrush, toothpaste, towel, and small sheet for the mat. They were strewn all over the filthy floor, indicating the lawful purpose the room existed to fulfill, was no longer its use.

Sleeping mat and a baggie full of hygiene items in hand, I entered what looked like an insane asylum. Two orange candy-striped inmates were screaming and cursing at each other, ready to fight over the only working telephone. They ignored the guard's momentary presence, and he ignored the fact they were ready to kill each other. At least sixty men in orange and white were screaming, shouting, gambling, cursing, exercising, and listening to a blaring TV hanging from the ceiling. There was not a place to kneel, much less lie down or place a sleeping mat. Never in my life had I witnessed such a scene.

I turned to ask the guard where to sleep, but he had fled. The mad house went on as if I were invisible.

The fifth floor of the Wake County Jail has four pods. They are named Blue, Yellow, Green, and Red, and cleverly painted in those color schemes. In their center stands a round dark glassed-in observation room where the jailers watch the madness in complete safety.

From the window and sliding door, I saw a similar scene in the Green pod, across from Blue. The Red pod was cater-cornered but partially visible around the guards' bubble.

It was disturbing to see how these small units held so many people. Each was tiered with one stairway going to the upper deck. The narrow ascent covered with men was barely passable. I was counting the number of cells when a man came over and said, "You look lost."

"I am," I responded. "Where do all of these men sleep? There seemed to be at least twice the bodies in here as places for them. I see only twenty-four rooms."

"Twenty-three, actually," he said. "They're superstitious here. There is no room thirteen anywhere in the building. There are more than twice the number of men as rooms. There are about sixty in here so far, but it's still early."

He was not kidding. The room numbers skipped from 12 to 14, and at least sixty men were in view, not counting those who were in rooms.

"I'm Michael Sprackland," he said, extending his hand. "The only place left to sleep is on the catwalk upstairs. The floor down here is covered. Come on. I'll get someone to slide his mat down a little so you can squeeze in." I looked up and around the balcony and sure enough, there were men littered all over the catwalk, sitting on their mats, hanging through the guardrail. The scene was reminiscent of an exaggerated Hollywood movie from the 1930s, of a prison or asylum; only this wasn't in black and white. It was so real it hurt my eyes and ears. There was apparently no separation between the extremely violent, sometimes violent, crazy, and innocent.

My new friend politely asked the stairway contingent to make way, and I followed him trying my best not to hit anyone. The mat dangling off my shoulder doubled the chances of incident.

The catwalk nearly encircled the pod. It hung off the wall on three and a half sides. Far from the stairs, Michael found a small gap and encouraged some to widen it and accommodate my mat. The parting of the floor closed, and fullness returned. Men were head-to-head and head-to-toe everywhere I looked. Downstairs, men were sitting on mats between the metal tables and chairs, both bolted to the concrete.

Other than the brightly colored prison suits and plastic, the scene could have been from a medieval, not an American, dungeon.

A fight broke out over the phone.

"Come on back downstairs if you like," Michael said, "and I'll tell you about this crazy place."

The facility was built for a maximum of twenty-three men, and if Michael's count was correct, we were two and a half times that number. I navigated through the bodies again and found him at a full table. A nice-looking gentleman asked someone to give me a seat. The man did so without question or comment, indicating respect. "Welcome to the Nut House. I'm Edwin from Angier, North Carolina," he said. "Where are you from?"

"I'm from North Carolina," I said, "but living in The Bahamas. Or at least I was."

"Bahamas? Damn, man. They're grabbing people from everywhere these days, aren't they?" Michael nodded in agreement.

Edwin was serving an exorbitant sentence for a small quantity of drugs, which was *enhanced* as he called it, due to an old pistol found by the police under the clothes dryer in his home during an illegal search.

Enhancements are artificial means by which government severely increases penalties and sentences under the *United States Sentencing Guidelines*, for elements not found by a jury and to which an individual has often not pled guilty.

The dealer who sold him the drugs gave Edwin up to get a time cut in his own sentence.

Michael said he was from Raleigh. He was charged with "conspiracy to launder money." Conspiracy, for those unfamiliar with it, is a body of law widely expanded during and since the Reagan era, which allows government to circumvent due process. The United States has had statutes for most of its history against a conspiracy to murder the president or to overthrow the government. Nations don't make it illegal to simply *think* about committing a crime and imprison those for doing so. Recent American conspiracy laws changed that.

Michael said, "Everybody ends up taking a plea," and Edwin nodded in agreement. "If you don't, then these guys will put you away for life. You can't fight them and win. They'll just keep on making up 'conspiracies' and keep making charges against you if you say you're going to trial. Nobody goes to trial any more, because you just can't win. I'm telling you the Feds win all the time, and it doesn't matter whether you're innocent or not. You have to take a plea."

More nodded in agreement.

I countered, "But neither my wife nor I ever knowingly broke any law. We don't understand what they've made up in the indictment. I can't just say I did something I didn't do and go to prison for it. That's wrong."

"You're right. It's wrong," Michael readily agreed. "It's not only wrong, it's against everything this country was supposed to be about. But that's the way it is. The sooner you understand it, the better off you'll be. When they come at you with a plea deal, which they will very soon, you'd better listen."

"I know it's crazy, but he's telling you the truth," Edwin said in support.

Michael continued, "They'll come at you more than once, usually two or three times. You don't have to take the first deal, but for God's sake, don't just blow them off. Tell them you'll think about it. Third visit is about it, though. That's the best deal you're going to get. If you don't take it, they'll destroy you, whether you did anything or not. They'll try to take the rest of your life. And these guys don't care about that. It's irrelevant to the Feds. They just want convictions, 'cause that's how they get raises. That's how they get paid."

The conversation overwhelmed me. More or less everything I believed about our judicial system was being challenged through personal experience. I was locked in a filthy mad house, though innocent, un-convicted, and pleading *not guilty* to the charges. I was granted bail, yet here I was in a completely different judicial district with no legal or constitutional authority, being told none of it mattered. I was going to prison, and my very expensive lawyer, whom my family hired to prepare for trial, had yet to discuss the case with me.

Hearing I was going to have to confess to uncommitted crimes and conspiracies just to avoid *life* in prison, however, was numbing. A few years, or life?

Michael asked, "Who is your judge?"

"I don't know. We live in the Middle District, but for some reason, they took us to Charlotte over in the Western District. Now they've brought us here to the Eastern District. I didn't think it was legal for them to do that."

"That doesn't make any sense at all," said Michael. "Something is going on. I've never heard of that."

I asked who their judges were. Both said, "W. Earl Britt."

Michael knew all about him. He said Judge Britt was a big Democrat, appointed to the bench by President Carter back in 1980. "Judge Britt has been on the bench here for nearly thirty years," he noted. Judge Britt took senior status in 1998, according to Michael, which usually precluded a judge from taking criminal cases at all, but he was hearing Michael's. Britt sent Edwin to prison before taking senior status, but was still handling his case years later.

I was a commissioner in the Department of Natural Resources under Governor Jim Martin in the 1980s and got a good taste of state politics in those days. It was a bare-knuckle, no-holds-barred, dirty business. I resigned in disgust before my term ended.

"It would really help if you were a Democrat. That matters down here," Michael said. "It matters to Judge Britt."

Having the name of former U.S. Attorney Samuel T. Currin, head of the Republican Party, on my indictment, would be less than helpful. All I could think of to say was it might be best for us not to have Judge Britt.

Michael's knowledge of his judge went way beyond anything he could glean from the news. He knew personal details and Britt's habits, which amazed me.

"How did you learn so much about this judge, Michael? You sound like you know him, personally."

"I ought to," Michael replied. "I've hung around his house all my life. I used to mow his lawn. He's been like a father in a lot of ways."

"How in the world did *that* happen?" I asked.

"My mother has been his court reporter forever. I've known him all of my life," he said.

"He can't be your judge, Michael. He'd have to recuse himself for sure if your mother works for him."

"I know that. He was supposed to, I guess, but you know how things work down here. Plus, I don't think he wanted to take a chance on my getting sentenced by one of the other judges. Some of them can be pretty nasty. Judge Britt will be fair because he knows me. The others might not."

We chatted awhile longer, but the day was catching up with me. The screaming from the crack heads, drunks, and crazies was more than I could yell over any longer. I bid my two new friends good night, and thanked Michael for his kindness in helping me find twelve squares of tile for my mat.

Depression is a great sedative, and the conversation definitely put me in that state.

Even with the profanity being screamed back and forth, and the TV blaring at an eardrum-shattering level, I found escape on a tiny piece of catwalk hanging over the madhouse.

CHAPTER 10

BOND HEARING – PART 2

"A universal principle as old as the law is that proceedings of a court without jurisdiction are a nullity and its judgment therein without effect either on person or property."

Norwood v. Renfield, 34 C 329; Ex parte Giambionini, 49 P. 732

Monday, April 24, 2006 – Wake County Jail,
Eastern District of North Carolina
4:40 a.m.

"**W**oltz! W-O-L-T-Z. You've got court. Get moving. The judge is waiting," a guard yelled from the door of Blue Pod. It took a minute to realize where I was. It took me longer to move. Sleep on the un-yielding floor cut off the nerves and blood circulation to my left leg and arm.

The zoo had quieted down a few minutes before the guard yelled to wake me for the 'waiting' judge. It wasn't five o'clock. The Wake County Jail had no line-ups and headcounts like Mecklenburg. They did nothing like that in Wake, but the pods were unattended by guards, and therefore, far more dangerous.

It was a twenty-three hour party house, complete with crack, cocaine, and marijuana. I saw it all being smoked and snorted the first night in Raleigh. They would light up by placing rolled pieces of aluminum foil in an electrical socket with a piece of paper between the prongs to catch flame. There was such unbelievable confusion and over-crowding, the guards did not want to be in the pods any more than we did. They would rather allow the drug-fest than try to stop it.

Somehow I urinated that morning without getting sick from the sights and smells of the communal toilet. There was nothing to throw up. I hadn't seen a half plate of food in a week.

A guard came to get me for the 'waiting' judge. He assembled a small chain gang, handcuffed together in a line. I was added, and we were marched to the elevator. We alternated snaking in and out, making steady movement towards a holding cell and waited.

Near seven a.m. a guard brought in breakfast bags. Knowing the drill, I shoved my way through. It was hardly worth the trouble, but every calorie was necessary. An hour and a half later, marshals showed up to transport us to the United States District Courthouse of Eastern North Carolina, Raleigh Division.

My wife was on the same van, but we were unable to speak. We were put in U.S. marshal's holding cells, once inside the courthouse. The crowded, loud, boisterous scene in the Eastern District bullpens was a replay of the chaos witnessed the week before in the Western District, except the Raleigh branch had windows across from the holding cells, providing a view of an older section of the state's capital city.

Upon entering the court, I saw Mother; my brothers, Jim and Thomas; Robert Cook; and assorted other friends and attorneys.

David B. Freedman, my attorney, came up and sat beside me at the last moment. "When can we meet so we can plan what we're going to do?" I asked.

"Shh! We'll talk later."

Just then, a pretty Hispanic woman came up to the defense table with copies of the Federal Criminal Code and Rules of Criminal Procedure. She was from the Public Defender's Office in Charlotte and came to stop the proceedings on our behalf. No one told her David Freedman had been hired to represent me.

"Mr. Freedman, I'm from the Public Defender's Office in Charlotte. I now understand you have been retained to represent Mr. Woltz, but you must be aware these proceedings cannot be held here in the Eastern District. This whole thing is illegal." She then showed David Freedman the rules and laws that clearly forbid what was about to happen, but he ignored her.

What *was* going on? This was an attorney in the United States government's employ saying this was all illegal? Why had my attorney not said so or done something to stop it?

"All rise," cried the bailiff, "Honorable W. Earl Britt presiding," and an elderly elfish-looking man in a bow tie appeared, mounting the large dais in a sweep.

"This is not good," I whispered to Vernice. She was sitting at the defendant's table with her lawyer, Don Tisdale. She had no idea what I was talking about, not being privy to the conversation with Michael and Edwin the night before or hearing the Public Defender. Judge Britt wasn't supposed to be hearing criminal cases after taking senior status, according to Michael. Here he was ready to adjudicate ours, though he had absolutely no jurisdiction to hear it in the Eastern District. Did he not know the law, or was he senile? Something was definitely up.

As we stood I sought my wife's hand under the table and squeezed it. Who would keep our children? How long would this horrible nightmare last? Would either of us ever be home with them?

David Freedman tugged at the sleeve of my prison suit. Everyone else had already taken a seat. I was lost in deep reflection and worry.

I noticed Britt's portrait hanging on the massive wooden wall of the courtroom behind him. Although it was further away than he, the portrait appeared larger. He began the proceedings by admonishing AUSAs Martens and Meyers against reviewing or revisiting anything said in Judge Keesler's court the week before.

"I've read it all and don't need to hear it again," the judge said nastily. He then proceeded to allow the government boys to drone on for close to an hour, reviewing and repeating the same nonsense from Charlotte. He permitted this without interruption. This time I *counted* the falsehoods. There were more than seventy outright untruths in their motion to revoke bond.

They claimed we were residents of The Bahamas, and would flee. They said I was a pilot years ago, and I would likely run out and steal a plane to fly away. They claimed I had a rich *Watchdog* with a million dollars to sweep in and protect me at a moment's notice.

At each untruth, I nudged David Freedman to respond or challenge them, but he refused to move an inch off the chair and told me, "Sshhh! Not now."

When the rant finally ended, David Freedman remained seated with his index fingers touching his lips, looking oddly bored.

My family paid him an initial retainer of $35,000 "to go to trial." My brother's contract with him made that the only stated expectation of his representation. It was very disconcerting. David could not or would not stand up for us at a bond hearing, one a Federal Public Defender proclaimed illegal. Not only did I have to worry about a pair of Assistant U.S. Attorneys who violated the law and a judge who participated in it, I had to worry about my own attorney.

Eight people had come from in state and out to help us, including two attorneys who questioned the jurisdiction and venue authority of Britt's Eastern District court in a Western District case, but none was allowed to speak. I now believe it was to prevent an on-the-record challenge of Judge Britt's lack of jurisdiction. As a matter of law, that would have required his court to prove its jurisdiction in the case before proceeding, which was something it could not do.

When I complained about this, David said Judge Britt wanted no redundancy from Judge Keesler's court, though lack of jurisdiction was not "redundancy" as there was no need to raise that issue in Charlotte. Charlotte had both jurisdiction and venue and it had attached there.

The ineffectual Freedman squandered our opportunities. No protest would be made, not one, before W. Earl's flowing black robe disappeared with him through the protective oak of his chambers doors.

Five minutes later, he returned to the courtroom and ordered us held in jail until trial. The rest of the day was a blur, with one exception. The crowd in the bullpen was mostly returned to the jail by the time Britt finished with us. Four of us remained.

Vernice was put in a cell at the end, well beyond the two others. I was in the adjacent cell and could hear them talking quietly. One was explaining to his friend the fine art of *snitching*.

According to the speaker, that is how the Feds got all or most of their victims. By being an informant or witness, his friend could get money and his sentence reduced by half. The teacher, a master snitch, boasted he was going into Judge Britt's court to get his third time-cut in the same case. His sentence of eighteen years had been reduced to nine, then four and a half, and he was getting his third time-cut to "time served." While in the Wake County Jail, he had made up cases for the Feds for over two years.

His first advice was to befriend those in the jail block. "Act friendly," he said. "Try to get them to start telling about themselves and things they've done in the past. Learn the details of their family and friends, their names, places they like to hang out, so the story sounds real."

All one had to do, according to the master snitch, was sound like he knew the person, and the Feds would take it from there. He said the U.S. Attorneys would coach him and write scripts to study and practice for testimony in court.

This is a federal crime under Title **18 U.S.C. §201(b)(3)-Bribery of witnesses-**

"Whoever directly or indirectly, corruptly gives, offers, or promises anything of value to any person, or offers or promises to give anything of value to any other person or entity, with intent to influence the testimony under oath or affirmation of such first-mentioned person as a witness upon a trial, hearing, or other proceeding, before any court; shall be fined under this title or imprisoned for not more than fifteen years, or both."

Snitches and informants are paid cash by government agents, and they are also paid by government prosecutors with time-cuts, a most frequent occurrence in cases today. U.S. Attorneys, however, have decided such things as money and freedom are not "of value," when they are the ones committing the crime. I cannot think of two things *more* valuable than money and freedom, and the law makes no exception for those who work for government. The statute applies equally to all.

Obviously, U.S. Attorneys are not going to bring charges against themselves. Moreover, there is no oversight or governing authority, like in many European nations, which have an Office of Ombudsman to prosecute government officials who break the law. Listening to the master snitch and his "Grasshopper" reminded me of a conversation years before with another U.S. Attorney, ironically my co-defendant, Samuel T. Currin.

Over dinner one night in Nassau in 2004, Vernice asked him, "So Sam, how did you like being U.S. Attorney?"

His face took on a pained expression, and he was momentarily upset. He told us before he died and met his "Maker," he intended to visit every prison in the Southeastern United States, and get down on his knees to beg the forgiveness of the men and women he put there.

Vernice and I were dumbfounded. It was one of those indelible moments. I was shocked by Sam's answer and had to know more. I asked why he would say something like that.

He told us as U.S. Attorney, he and his staff made up charges, fabricated evidence, gave informants time-cuts in exchange for telling lies on the stand, falsified evidence, hid evidence, and did any and everything necessary to win. He admitted putting a lot of people in prison that had absolutely no business being there, and said he was ashamed of it.

I asked why he would have done this, and he said that is how the system is structured. His professional advancement was based on two things: how many convictions a prosecutor got each year, and how many years their targets were sentenced. Nothing else mattered. Sam said they did anything they had to in order to accomplish those ends.

I asked what happened if they realized a suspected target was innocent. Would the prosecutor recognize and correct the mistake? How could there be no recognition and an effort to do the right thing?

"That's the problem with our justice system," Sam replied. "It just doesn't work that way anymore." Sam assured us anyone trying to do 'the right thing' would not work long in a U.S. Attorney's office.

"It is all about winning convictions and long sentences," he said.

A silence fell on the table that night and the pall never lifted.

Little did we know Sam's sins would come back and smite the three of us. The same methods he employed against others for his own advancement and personal gain would be deployed against him.

In the future we three would be destroyed by our association, Sam's legacy and his successors' zealous attempts to make their own mark as Sam had once done.

Sam went from hunter to hunted, and would soon be a trophy of two young AUSAs, the next generation of ruthless prosecutors whom Sam helped spawn. He would be slain by his own cruel sword and eaten by his own.

I was brought out of my deep thoughts and remembrances by Vernice's voice calling from a cell down the corridor.

"Howell? What does this all mean?" she said through her sobs of anguish. "Are they going to keep us down here in Raleigh? What's going to become of us? When will I see the children again?" The men next door went silent.

"Why are they doing this to us, Howell?"

Her unanswerable questions were from a mother's broken heart and my silence was the only response I could muster for her absent children.

I had no answers other than the one Sam Currin gave. We were there to add to the reputation and pay-grade of two ambitious young prosecutors who wanted to be the next Elliott Spitzer or Alberto Gonzalez.

We were returned to the Wake County Jail in chains. After the usual long wait in holding cells, we were taken to our respective cellblocks to sleep, on the floor, with the day's collection of arrestees.

Michael and Edwin were waiting for me in Blue pod, but the report to new friends would have to wait until morning. My expression told the day's outcome. I made it to the catwalk, balled up on the thin mat and covered against the waking day of night. I once again asked the universe why this was happening, and soon found escape in sleep.

CHAPTER 11

OUT OF THE FRYING PAN AND INTO THE FIRE

"Excessive bail shall not be required, nor excessive fines imposed, nor cruel and unusual punishments inflicted."

Amendment 8, United States Constitution

April 25, 2006 – Eastern, Middle, and Western Districts of North Carolina

My wife and I were taken back to Charlotte in U.S. marshals' vans after a long stop at the Raleigh-Durham International Airport (RDU). One of the marshals tried to give me a religious tract about telling the truth.

"You need to be giving that to the U.S. attorneys, not me, " I replied.

We were delivered to a private fixed-base operation at RDU, in a van full of the chained and hapless.

Almost all federal prisoners are sent to Oklahoma City, Oklahoma by a private air carrier, Prison Air Transport Service (PATS). Although I have found no legitimate reason for this, men and women are shipped there to spend days, weeks or months in a detention center after sentencing. They are brought from every state in the nation. Almost all are flown back to the place from which they came, most likely the same airport, according to many, and carted to a nearby prison.

Most of the actions for which people now go to federal prison were simply considered bad behavior until recent years and correctly deemed to be outside of Washington's purview. Drug possession, a myriad of technical statutes concocted under the interstate commerce clause, and the Reagan-era "conspiracy" statutes now fill federal prisons to an average of 130 percent of maximum capacity. Prison was once reserved for those who committed real crimes, such as murder, rape, robbery or aggravated assault. Now there are over 14,000 laws attached to prison penalties. Quite a change.

The wait on the RDU tarmac allowed me to overhear several conversations. Some told of going to Oklahoma on more than one occasion and one was going for a third time. The entire business resembled a very expensive scam. People were making money transporting federal prisoners all over the nation with little to show for it.

Prison Air Transport Service (PATS) or "Con-Air" as it is called, employs private contractors under the U.S. Marshal Service to carry prisoners. The idea originated when an old jet was donated by the FAA to the marshals' service years ago. The expanded service, officially known as JPATS, is run by a private airline with ten craft, carrying 350,000 prisoners a year, according to Wikipedia. Old 737's, MD-80s or leased jets from long-bankrupt Pan Am, rumbled into RDU the days I was there, to discharge and pick up human cargo. Every seat was full. One U.S. marshal piloted the plane and another was in back, but everyone else had on a PATS badge, meaning they were a private contractor.

Each week the plane came through, marshals' vans, county sheriff dog box trucks, and private prison buses from across the state converged on the FBO (fixed base operation) at RDU to exchange prisoners. Watching from the marshals' van the first trip, it was shocking to see shackled citizens getting on and off dilapidated planes. Only the extreme wasteful absurdity could exceed the indignity.

We were eventually swapped to U.S. marshals from Charlotte and returned to the Mecklenburg County Jail in the district of jurisdiction. Processing took nearly two hours longer the second time than it had the week before, though all our information was on file.

We were re-photographed, re-finger-printed, re-questioned, re-manhandled, and re-booked. The guards would not let us sit together, but we could see each other across the large room. Our eyes fixed. I blankly wondered when we would have this opportunity again.

After processing, I was escorted to the second floor and put in a tiny pod designed for a handful of medical inmates. There were eight double-bunk beds and tables for just sixteen, but the place was wall-to-wall men. The only available floor space for the sleeping mat was beside the toilets. No one in my family or the world knew where to find me, and the fake PIN number for phone access was no closer to working than before. I was dying to know what happened to our children, but had no way of finding out.

A Sumo-wrestling sized man screamed karate noises as I entered the room. He made the sounds with each chess piece move. The men sleeping on the floor in the bathroom corner made room. My new neighbors were an assortment of vagrants, homeless, drunks, and panhandlers rounded up for the night.

These were the same people I ignored on street corners and urban thoroughfares the world over. I was now sleeping with them in one of the worst jails in the region.

The one to my left croaked, "Scooter's the name. Want something to read?"

"Thanks," I said, taking from Scooter a well-worn Robert Tannenbaum novel about corruption in the justice system.

Scooter's diction was excellent, and other than his burned-out voice, he could pass for a regular guy in any setting. We chatted, and I was fascinated. His real name was Henry Miller, like the author, he said. "He wrote the *Tropic of Cancer* and *The Tropic of Capricorn*," which I'd never read, but heard of. Scooter could tell stories too.

He was the child of two desperate alcoholics and grew up fending for himself on the streets. Henry was a prolific consumer of the written word, and there was little about which he did not know. His knowledge was expressed casually, with no intention to impress.

Occasionally, he would break into a boisterous laugh, which was infectious. I completely forgot my woes and worries while talking to Henry. He spoke candidly of the harsh liquids he had poured down his throat; some of these partially robbed him of speech.

Henry "Scooter" Miller was an urban Henry David Thoreau, and downtown Charlotte was his Walden Pond. He lived where and as he wished and followed no man's bidding. On occasion, when in basic need or tired of being a sage, he would buy a tall can of cold beer with donated funds and stand on a corner, sipping it openly, taunting a police cruiser, demanding it stop.

If they hesitated to arrest him, Henry threatened, "to throw up all over the back seat of their police car" and demanded a ride to jail.

"Works every time!" Henry shouted, breaking into his high-pitched laugh.

Gradually others joined our company. Garfield was a young gymnast/drug dealer who grew up as an Air Force brat. His military parents were both drug addicts. He saw bases all over the world and dealt drugs from age thirteen to support them.

David Wu was a gregarious Vietnamese businessman whom the Feds were holding because he wouldn't sign a guilty plea to an uncommitted crime. The Feds couldn't take him to trial, as they had no evidence. David would sit there until he either pled guilty to something, or they found time-cut artists to testify against him. I learned from another Vietnamese gentleman, John Nguyen, they later arrested his wife for leverage and forced him to plead guilty so as to let her go.

The huge Sumo-sized man came by too. His name was Terry Streit, but unlike a Sumo wrestler, there was no hair knot on the back of his head, just a patch of solid flesh, four inches wide.

His voice, in contrast to his size, was child-like in pitch and his manner extremely polite. Sentences all started or ended with "Sir." He also offered books and sundries.

Garfield, the gymnast, entertained us by doing amazing feats along with flips and handstands between chairs and tables.

A friendly Hispanic fellow told me I needed a haircut, which was true, and shortly thereafter, I was barbered, given books and food, and enjoyed a thoroughly fascinating evening with new friends. Not many nights or jail pods would be this rewarding, and I was grateful for it after the violence of Raleigh.

I wanted to brush my teeth, but when asked for hygiene items, the jailer said, "We're out."

Scooter, gave me an *indigent pack*, which was for those, like he, who had no funds in their account. It contained everything I needed: a comb, toothpaste, toothbrush, soap, and a small deodorant. Everyone else bought on commissary, which I could not do as I had no funds.

It was quite touching, actually, but I felt a wash of guilt. I'd stepped over and avoided such men for years and couldn't recall ever giving them the time of day, yet here was one giving me easily half of his worldly possessions without a moment's reflection. Some piece of my faith was missing or not fully present, for each soul, including these, was part of the Creation. I was to respect and treat one as such, as brothers or part of nature, for they could be the forest through which I walked in the absence of the trees.

Their kindness was overwhelming. Comfortably successful in my world, I separated from others, mistakenly viewing myself above many. I wondered if I deserved their generosity.

Henry and I read books until early morning. Mr. Sumo wrestler, Terry Streit, snored so loudly it shook the small pod with thunder, making sleep more or less impossible, but I felt I had made acquaintances and seen more of what life was about.

CHAPTER 12

THE OTHER SHOE HITS
THE FLOOR

"The prosecutor is an officer of the court whose duty is to present a forceful and truthful case to the jury, not to win at any cost."

United States v. Filion, 335 F.3d. 119 (2ⁿᵈ Cir. 2003)

April 26, 2006 – Western District of North Carolina

I sought assistance from one of the guards, Mr. Federson, on the PIN number for the phone. He seemed more sympathetic towards his captives than most, and that perception proved correct.

About a half hour later, I had a working number.

I was able to reach my sister-in-law in Florida. The person receiving the call was required to sign up for the expensive private telephone system before a call could be made. She told me the children were safe. Robert Cook had taken our oldest son, Chris, to live with him. He delivered our youngest, John, to Jacksonville, to stay with her. Robert also saw to it John's young friend flew back to Nassau. His parents read of our arrest on the front page of *The Nassau Guardian* the morning after and were frantic. My sister-in-law spent over $600 the first couple of weeks on calls from Vernice and me, checking on the children. We had no idea she was paying $25.00 per call.

Phone systems are a large source of revenue for jails and prisons. Jails take a handsome cut from these companies such as Evercom and ITI. One guard told me that prison management took other payments, in form of kickbacks, for the service. Everywhere I looked, someone was making money off of us. We had to buy everything we needed at exorbitant prices from Aramark, a private prison contractor. Everything we touched, used, or were fed, came from some private supplier at a profit. The term, "prison industry," took on a new meaning for me.

Shortly after I had made my first call, a gruff voice yelled, "Woltz! Pack your shit now, and get your ass in the slider. Now, Woltz! Move it!"

I bid adieu to my new friends and joined the overweight deputy in the enclosed glass slider. Off we went to pod 6800, about which I was already warned. It was called *the murderers pod*, and it was called that for a reason.

Unlike the other pods in Mecklenburg, 6800 had no podium or visible guard, just a spooky-looking, one-way mirrored wall housing two officers hidden from view. Everything is automated. There are fifty-four solitary confinement cells on two tiers. Other than the few faces staring through the tiny windows in the cell doors, no one was visible when I entered.

The cell door to number 34 on the upper level popped open, and once inside, a voice came over the in-cell speaker telling me to close the door. Another frisson shot up my back, just like the first night, but this was somehow worse. I was losing human contact.

Cell 34 consisted of 312 concrete blocks and a tiny metal cot crammed beside a postage-stamp sized table with a swing-out chair underneath. There was a steel sink/toilet combination, with hot and cold-water taps, though only cold worked. The sink water drained directly into the toilet. The ceiling was quite high, maybe twelve feet. Prisoners are required to have a certain number of *cubic* feet of living space. Rather than waste ground footage that could be used by the occupant, the mandate appears to be fulfilled by increasing ceiling height.

Boredom and depression, a prisoner's constant companions, quickly set in. I could not stop thinking of my children or their mother. She was in solitary confinement just two floors below. We had entered Hell.

CHAPTER 13

DEALIN' WITH THE DEVIL – PART 1

"The defendant's decision to enter a *not guilty* plea carries with it the expectation that a full-scaled attack on the state's case will be conducted by the attorney. Anything short of this expectation compromises the defendant in that effort to achieve his or her primary objective, a *not guilty* determination. The attorney should not unilaterally change this expectation. If a strategy is developed that omits some challenges, that matter should be explained to the defendant and approval of the particular strategy should be obtained."

North Carolina Criminal Procedures, Ethical and Practical Concerns When Representing, p. 55

April 27, 2006 9:13 a.m. – Custodial Interrogation Room – Mecklenburg County Jail – Western District of North Carolina

Mornings started later in the murderer's pod. We were allowed out of solitary confinement at certain times and for meals, though that was not consistent. Sometimes we were fed through a slot in the door affectionately known as *the bean hole* for days at a time, especially around holidays. The guards usually allowed us out for a couple of hours prior to lunch and dinner and then in the evening about 8:30 p.m. for an hour or two. The rest of the time was spent in the solitude of our individual cells.

The inmates were far less friendly. Many, if not most, were there for charges of murder or seriously violent crimes, and most had been there for a long time. The prosecutor's hand was definitely at play. My being there was not an accident. I was taken out of the cellblock early on the morning of April 27, for what they called a *contact visit*. I had no idea what that was or why I was being taken.

David Freedman had not met with me or shown any interest in learning about the case, and I had not seen him outside of a courthouse. I tried to call him time and again once I had a working PIN, but he refused to take calls or to set up a phone on the jailhouse system. I found it odd that a man who represented himself as "the best criminal defense attorney in North Carolina," did not have his office or cell phone connected to his client's jail for pre-trial communication. There was only one reasonable explanation for not accepting such calls, I thought. Perhaps he did not want our conversations monitored. Maybe he was my "contact" visit. Maybe he had a plan.

The guard took me by elevator to the second floor. There was a large metal door beside it which the sergeant opened using an oversized key painted with a red dot. I was thoroughly frisked and patted down. Another guard entered the small hallway, and the door behind us locked again. Only then was the door at the other end of the hallway opened. We entered an area with four meeting rooms. The guard said, "Stand by the door until they're ready for you."

Who were "they" I wondered?

Walking toward the room, I glimpsed Doug Curran, the FBI agent who arrested us, not to be confused with my co-defendant, Sam Currin. I also thought I saw the prosecutor, Matthew Martens, but was not sure. The guard left me beside the door, out of their view, to wait. Once still, I heard Martens talking excitedly about Sam Currin and Judge Britt, the man who revoked our bond the week before in Raleigh.

His conversation got my quick attention. AUSA Martens bragged to the assemblage of orchestrating Judge Britt to revoke our bond in the Eastern District with the Clerk of Court, and admitted to choosing him due to his bias in favor of the prosecution.

"Judge Britt and Sam Currin are blood-feud enemies of thirty years!" Martens almost shouted. "I can't believe we got him to take the case!" His audience broke out in laughter.

Matt Martens was admitting to *judge shopping* for W. Earl Britt. His crime violated my Sixth Amendment right to an "impartial tribunal" as had our transportation to Britt's court and district, according to the federal Public Defender who came to stop it.

The deputy noticed my listening, and knocked on the door to let them know I was outside. We were told to come in. I was dumbfounded. Sitting beside AUSA Martens was my own attorney, David B. Freedman. He had been as entertained as the rest by Martens' crow.

Before sitting down, I asked David, "Aren't we going to have a chance to talk alone?" I was anxious to discuss what I just heard and ask what he intended to do about it.

"I don't think that's necessary. Once you hear what we've come up with, I think you'll agree that isn't needed," Freedman said.

"We need to talk alone, David. Now."

Martens picked up the conversation. "Mr. Woltz, I know these last several days have been really rough for you and your wife. But you're not who we're interested in. We are sure that you can help us, but you're not our target."

He paused, smiled broadly and said slowly, "How would you like to get off of this merry-go-round? Just step off, and be done with it. Hmm?"

A million thoughts went through my head from strangling the "best criminal defense lawyer in North Carolina" to walking out of the room.

Half a dozen government men smiled at me as if they were my friends. They were waiting for me to answer this loaded question. I could have kicked Freedman for having no chance to speak privately or be warned of the meeting. What was he doing? They were giving me no time to make an informed decision, and apparently, my suspicions were correct. Freedman was definitely working with them, not for me. This was our first meeting, and he was holding it in front of the enemy after I pled not guilty to the charges and ordered him to prepare for trial.

"What do you think, Mr. Woltz?" Martens said. "You'd like that, wouldn't you?"

I had mailed Freedman a line-by-line rebuttal on the back of the indictment on April 19, just eight days before, telling him how we could prove every charge false. I gave him the names of witnesses and contacts to call. But I also remembered what Michael Sprackland and Edwin told me in Raleigh about hearing them out. Perhaps I should at least listen to what Martens had to say.

I said as non-committedly as possible. "What are you proposing?"

Martens pointed to David Freedman to answer that question.

"Howell, I've been doing this a long time, and I've got to tell you, what Matt is offering you is really unbelievable. It is without a doubt, the best 'deal' I've ever seen for someone facing the charges and number of years in prison you are."

"But I didn't do anything! I just came up here to help them, and they grabbed me. I don't even understand why I'm here."

"OK. OK. Calm down. That really isn't important right now," Freedman cooed as an adult would to quiet a child's tantrum. "Let's put that aside for the moment."

How could charges, provably false, be "not important"?

"But how can we put that aside?"

"Howell, stop," Freedman interrupted. "Hear us out before you say any more."

"Us?" At least he was admitting he was part of their team.

"Suppose I told you we've come to an agreement whereby this all ends, or as Matt said, 'You can get off the merry-go-round right now.' Now keep in mind that you've been indicted by a grand jury."

"But–" I tried to interject. David held up his hand.

"Let me finish. This is not going away. We've come to an agreement, and as I said, it is an unbelievably good deal you're being offered, where this can end soon and with as little pain as possible."

I wanted to run out of the room, but couldn't. I didn't even want to hear what he was going to say.

"Matt and I have agreed to this. We only need your approval."

What? He hadn't even talked to me, and he'd already cut a deal with the prosecutor?

"Now as you've probably already figured out, you're going to have to take a charge, and admit to having done something. Something small," he whispered.

"But I didn't do any of this!" I blurted. "They've got to know that if they've done any investigation at all!"

FBI Agent Curran jumped in and said, "A grand jury sure thinks you've done something!"

"Then somebody had to have lied!" I shot back immediately.

Martens raised his hand to silence both of us. "Go on Mr. Freedman," he said.

"OK. Howell, you're going to have to plead guilty to something."

"Something. Anything, really," Martens interjected.

What was this all about? It didn't even matter what I pled guilty to, just that I did? I was reminded of what Eugene said about the old Dominican man these same people held in Mecklenburg for years. Eugene said, "If they let him go after all of this time, he could sue them for false imprisonment, so they've got to just wear him down now until he agrees to plead guilty to something, anything really, so they can justify holding him."

Freedman jumped back in before I could speak, "But let's leave that for a moment. Let me tell you what we've worked out. There are four items. First of all, your wife can go free immediately, if you agree to help the government. Second, there will be no forfeiture of any assets. That's got to please you."

"What a great deal," I thought. I'll not get robbed by the United States government for something I never did?

"Third, you'll serve little or no time. You help them and you're almost home now."

"Wait. You just said 'little' or 'no'," I interrupted. "Which is it? It's already too late for 'no' time. I'm in jail now."

"That's part of what we'll discuss, but let me finish," Freedman said. "The fourth part is that there will be no new charges of any kind made against you. This is the end of it, if you agree to help them against Sam Currin."

"Let me make sure that I understand what you're saying, David. You want me to help them against Currin, which I came to do voluntarily. In return for doing so, I'm guaranteed: one, that my wife goes free *now*; two, there is no forfeiture of our assets; three, I serve little or 'no' time; and, four, no new charges of any kind will be added. Is that correct?"

"That's pretty much it," Freedman responded, "but keep in mind that you will have to plead guilty to some small charge."

"Why?" I asked. "Why do I have to plead guilty to something I didn't do? They know I didn't do anything. I was on my way here to help them on an issue I reported."

Martens took the tag from his partner on this one, "First off, we not only want your help with Currin, but also his client, Jeremy Jaynes. We'll expect you to testify against both of them, and it will add to your credibility with the jury if you've pled guilty to something and say that you were working with them. It will make you much more believable."

"But I *didn't* know what they were doing, and you know that, Mr. Martens. You have the information in your file. I know you do, because I sent it to you."

We had documents and affidavits from people involved with Currin and his clients in a case from the Supreme Court of The Bahamas, where the defendants admitted we knew nothing about Jaynes' activities, as they had done his legwork without our knowledge.

"I can't look at that. It's under seal," Martens quipped.

This was the same government official who made up false charges, forced witnesses to commit perjury so he could get an indictment against us, and kidnapped my wife and me on those false charges in another federal district because our own home district would not participate in his 'sham prosecution.' Martens had lied and/or suborned perjury to a grand jury to get the indictment, told a federal judge by my count seventy-six mistruths and outright lies in an attempt to deny us our constitutional right to bail. He then went judge shopping in a foreign district to rob of us that bail, and took us to a foreign district with no legal authority over our case to do it. Now, all of a sudden, he was too ethical to look at exculpatory information that proved we had no knowledge of, or involvement in, any of the criminal activity he was alleging.

"It's on the Internet, Mr. Martens. I'd hardly call that 'confidential information'," I replied as calmly as possible.

The meeting was coming off the rails. Freedman jumped back in to save his partner.

"Now, Howell, this isn't going to get us anywhere. Calm down, and listen to me. If you go to trial, you're risking spending the rest of your life in prison. The government's conviction rate is ninety-nine percent. You need to listen to Matt. Let's leave the part about the charge for a moment, but let me assure you, you need to hear this, and give it serious consideration."

I wanted to ask how any honest government could possibly win ninety-nine percent of the time, but the question was the answer. An *honest* government couldn't.

And I was living proof of how they did it. Kidnapping, extortion, perjured testimony to grand juries, threats, taking loved ones as hostages, and holding you in jail until you cry "Uncle." I tried to rein in myself, get calm, and ask the obvious question.

"How does my being guilty of something, or being a convicted *felon*, possibly make me more credible with *anyone*? That makes absolutely no sense. The opposite would be true. Do you think the jury is more likely to believe someone who says he's a crook? I don't get that at all."

Freedman and Martens exchanged glances; they faltered on that one. There was no credible answer. Martens wanted another win and my attorney, David Freedman, was going to help him get it. Credibility with the jury was the last thing about which they were concerned, as there would be no jury if I pled guilty. My radar was going wild, but I also did not want to lose the conversation if they were agreeing to let us go home to our children and not steal everything we had. I did not know it at the time, but they had already locked down all of our business and personal accounts to prevent us from accessing funds for attorneys.

After a silence, David said, "I'll try to explain that later, Howell. You're just going to have to trust me for right now. That's the deal, and I've got to tell you, it's the best you're ever going to get, and it's certainly the best I've ever heard of."

From Michael and Edwin's stories in Raleigh and Eugene's in Charlotte, I tended to believe that was true, as wrong and odious as government's methodology may be. Go home instead of jail, take a minor charge, and get our lives back. I was tempted.

"Let me see a copy of your agreement," I said.

Freedman and Martens again exchanged glances, as if waiting for the other to speak first.

"David?" I said warily.

"I don't have a copy with me," he responded.

"But this agreement has been reduced to *writing*, right?" I pressed.

They looked at each other again.

"I mean, you do have letters back and forth or e-mails, or something memorializing this four-point deal, right?"

Freedman answered, "Yes. It has been memorialized."

"In my world, David, *memorialized* means that something has been reduced to writing. Is that what you are saying? Are you, as my attorney, telling me that I am covered on this?"

"Yes. Yes, you, you're covered," he answered somewhat hesitantly.

"If that is so, what do we do next?" I asked.

Martens took the tag again from his partner, "If we're in agreement, Mr. Woltz, then we'd like to ask you a few questions, now that we have that out of the way."

Freedman looked greatly relieved.

Rather than answering Martens, I said to David, "I'm counting on you. If you're telling me that you've got this deal in writing and I'm *covered*, then I don't have a problem with that, but what assurances do I have that what I say won't be used to make up more false charges against me?"

David reached in his briefcase and produced two copies of a Non-Attribution Agreement, but only after I asked the question.

"We have an agreement, which I've also got to tell you, Howell, is the best that I think I've ever seen. You can even incriminate yourself without repercussion. You're free to talk openly, once this is signed."

I took a copy of the agreement from him and scanned it quickly. It was dated April 21, the day after the original bond hearing. David's signature was already on it, dated April 24, three days before this meeting. What the hell was going on? How could he have done this without talking to me?

"The items you and Mr. Martens just promised me are not here, David. I want to see them first before we do this."

"You're just going to have to trust me on that, Howell. All of these people are here to talk to you now, today. I'm not sure we can get a delay. This is your one opportunity."

With that, David looked at his watch, and said, "Look, Howell, I've got something really important to do this morning. I promise you all of this is set. But I've got to go, so let's get this signed so you can start helping these gentlemen, all right?"

"Something really important," I thought to myself. I again said, "I want a copy of these four items you told me were *memorialized* before we move ahead."

David promised to send a copy to my brother Jim and me, as well as the executed Non-Attribution Agreement when he got back to his office that afternoon. He packed his things without fanfare or feeling. He was prepared to leave without getting Martens to write down the four items. What I wanted in writing, Freedman was content to promise, after the fact. Was he just going to leave me after I had told him I wanted everything in writing first?

What I thought paid for legal services in preparation for trial ($35,000), paid instead for the likes of a cameo actor working a cheap gig acting as government's cheerleader and salesman. I never talked to David outside of the courthouse, and now he was abandoning me to half a dozen or so federal agents and attorneys, without the assistance or advice of counsel.

"David, I'm counting on your word that all of this is set, and I am protected."

He stood up to leave, "Howell, you need to focus on how you can help these men now. You just made a very good deal. Now it's time for you to do your part. You're covered. This is almost over. But I've really got to go now."

I tried again to stop him until I got proof of their deal, but he bolted out the door.

My attorney sold me down the river and made a deal with the prosecutor without ever talking to me or asking a single question other than how I pled at arraignment, which was *not guilty*. He knew nothing about the case or me. As soon as the door closed, the mood palpably changed. The wolves that remained dropped pleasantries and pursued prey.

One spoke and said, "I'm Scott Schiller with the IRS. I'm the agent on this case." He and the others then told me of the testimony I was expected to give against Sam Currin and his client. I knew nothing of what they spoke. The events described either happened after we resigned as trustees or were unknown to us.

At the bond revocation, I learned from the prosecutors' rant that this Agent Schiller sent two con men, also known as "undercover agents," to The Bahamas, to pose as potential clients. I remembered their visit, but our due diligence department felt they were interested in skirting U.S. law. They wired $50,000 to the firm, assuming they would be accepted as clients, and we returned it. Not a single transaction ever took place. Not only were their funds returned, our company ordered the attorney who referred them, Rick Graves, now listed on the indictment as a co-defendant, to inform them, in writing, they were rejected as clients.

Mr. Graves dutifully notified them their business was not accepted. We considered the matter closed, never suspecting these con artists were sent to entrap us. Fortunately, they were refused as clients, so no 'conspiracy' was possible. Had one existed, we clearly withdrew from it by refusing their money and business, which made the charge legally impossible.

Unable to entrap us into criminal conduct so we might be charged and detained as witnesses in a semi-legal way, we were kidnapped and charged with the crime they attempted to create as though it actually happened.

The bizarre Kafkaesque world I entered would only get darker.

CHAPTER 14

DEALIN' WITH THE DEVIL – PART 2

"Counsel must be present at custodial interrogation."

Edwards v. Arizona, **451 US 477, 68 L.Ed. 2d 564,
101 S.Ct. 665**

**"Zealous representation demands that an attorney
diligently prepare a theory of the defense and fully
investigate every aspect of the case. Every potential witness
must be interviewed. The attorney's failure to conduct a
thorough investigation and conduct pre-trial discovery
violates the Rules of Professional Responsibility and the
Sixth Amendment."**

Kimmelman v. Morrison, **477 US 365, 106 S.Ct. 2574**

April 27, 2006 – 9:45 a.m. – Western District of North Carolina

My lawyer left me alone in a custodial interrogation without the benefit of counsel. He jumped the coop before the first question was asked, to go do something "really important." The moment I was without counsel, the session became illegal.

I now faced both assistant U.S. attorneys who violated Federal law by taking us to a foreign jurisdiction for bond revocation before a *shopped* judge who had no legal authority in our case. They were joined by the IRS, Agent David Scott Schiller, who admittedly committed an international crime by attempting an entrapment scheme on foreign soil, without that nation's permission.

The actions and words of FBI Agent Doug Curran indicated no investigation of the case on his part, or he would have cause to place Martens, Meyers and Schiller under arrest instead of us. The prosecutors violated multiple criminal statutes in these actions. Had they been prosecuted just for the crimes committed as of April 27, their sentences could be as high as forty-five years each by statutory law, if found guilty.

Five of them and one me. Six of them if one were to count *my* absent attorney. That apparently seemed fair.

Not quite ready to let it all go, I asked, "What on earth does any of this have to do with my wife and me?"

"OK. I admit it's a bit of a stretch," said Agent Schiller, smiling, "but it doesn't really matter, does it? You're working with us now."

Just hearing those words made me feel dirty.

"Let me make sure I've got this right on your *conspiracy* allegation, Mr. Schiller. You've just ruined our lives over a transaction that *never* happened because your con men were rejected by our due diligence staff," I said.

"They're *agents* not *con men*," Schiller said briskly.

"In a foreign jurisdiction where you had no authority to be? No, they were con men. And your charge," I continued, "is basically saying that if we *had* accepted your men as clients, which we did not, that a transaction may have taken place. Is that right?"

"Yes," he responded.

"And if a transaction *had* taken place, which it could not have, because your con men couldn't pass our due diligence."

"They're *agents* not *con men!*" he interrupted again, more harshly.

"If they *had* passed our due diligence and *had* this transaction which never occurred been profitable, then a trust, which was subject to our sole discretion, *might* have declared a distribution of some of these non-existent profits? Is that it so far?"

Agent Schiller nodded, clearly becoming angry.

"And had these con men, being U.S. citizens, decided not to report these monies, that would somehow have been our fault instead of theirs?" I asked.

"Agents. They're agents!" he said sternly, any trace of humor gone.

He then hissed like a snake and said, "But as I said, none of that matters anymore. You're working for *us* now!"

Like Dante's *Inferno*, I was sinking into Hell, expecting at any moment to see old Ugolino, the one who ate his children and grandchildren, down in the Ninth Circle. My impertinence reached its limit. The rest of the morning was spent in desperate search for wrongdoing by which to create a crime to therefore attach a charge that may have substance.

Agent Curran, clueless, flailed about trying to make me confess to charges made up by his peers in the Office of the U.S. Attorney. No one had the courtesy to let him in on the gag or tell him they were invented.

And why did they need for me to *confess* to things I never did, if we had a 'deal'?

None of it made any sense, and my lawyer was not there to ask any of these questions. That's why such interrogations were deemed illegal by the U.S. Supreme Court, I suppose. These men could now say I said anything they wanted, and it would be my word against theirs.

I finally said, "We didn't do anything and you know it."

Martens watched this interchange quietly, but couldn't resist. "Oh you've done something, Mr. Woltz," he smiled. "We believe that all of you out there have done *something*, we just haven't gotten around to you yet."

This remark chilled my soul. I truly believe he was trained to think this way, and adopted that view as representative of the U.S. justice system. I realized at that moment, however, all he had to do was get Sam Currin or his clients to claim *I* knew what they were doing in exchange for a time cut in *their* sentences, and I, not they, would go to jail for a conspiracy that never was.

The guard knocked on the door and told them it was time for my midday "feeding".

I later learned just how far down the road of injustice AUSA Martens' view has taken America. According to the BNA Criminal Law Reporter, May 19, 2010 issue (Vol. 87, No.7), "The U.S. Department of Justice estimates that 71 million people—approximately 25 percent of the American population—have a criminal record." That statistic, one of every four Americans, indicates AUSA Matthew Martens' view has prevailed for some time now in the *land of the free*, and I was on my way to being added to that number, if he had anything to do with it.

CHAPTER 15

DEALIN' WITH THE DEVIL – PART 3

"The right to effective assistance of counsel is the right of the accused to require the prosecution's case to survive the crucible of meaningful adversarial testing...The adversarial process protected by the Sixth Amendment requires that the accused have counsel acting in the role of an advocate."

United States v. Cronic, **466 US 648, L ed 2d 657, 104 S.Ct. 2039**

April 27, 2006 – 12:30 p.m. – Western District of North Carolina

I was dreading the afternoon session with the agents and prosecutors and getting angrier by the minute at David Freedman for abandoning me.

The picture had fully materialized. Charges were fabricated to keep us in the United States. I was to be a "smoking gun" witness against their targets, Sam Currin and Jeremy Jaynes. IRS Agent David "Scott" Schiller said so in the morning session and laughed at me for being so upset about it. AUSAs Martens and Meyers cobbled a case together in early April once I agreed to come to North Carolina to assist them, and no doubt, lied to a grand jury and cajoled them into rubber stamping the indictment. The grand jury was held only ten days before the scheduled meeting, according to the date on the indictment, explaining why it had the appearance of being so sloppily thrown together. It had been. They did this so I could not return to The Bahamas, according to IRS Agent Schiller.

"And your attorney has now abandoned you." He laughed at me about that as well. He was gleeful, even proud of his actions, and not the least bit embarrassed, for he willingly bragged of what he did. I noticed FBI Agent Curran looking quizzically at him when he said these things. Curran was catching on as well.

Agent Schiller also admitted they made up charges against my wife so she could be held as leverage on me, or as he put it, "To ensure your *full* cooperation."

This sham was not happening in some unfortunate country absent an operative system of justice, but in the United States of America, and my own attorney was aiding and abetting.

They were forthright about *who* and *what* they were after. They wanted former U.S. Attorney Samuel T. Currin and his clients, but I was beginning to suspect they would go for any scalp in a pinch.

If AUSA Martens' earlier account concerning Judge W. Earl Britt being Sam Currin's "blood-feud enemy of thirty years," was accurate, then the conspiracy to deprive our constitutional rights extended two federal jurisdictions away and to a senior federal district court judge.

My attorney, FBI and IRS agents, and AUSA Kurt Meyers all heard Martens' admission of criminal conduct and did nothing about it. They, not us, were involved in a conspiracy. They had an obligation to report what they heard. The legal term for this is *misprision of a felony*, and it is a crime under The Federal Criminal Code, Title 18 U.S.C. §4.

The animosity between Sam Currin and W. Earl Britt started in 1980 when, according to AUSA Martens, Currin and Senator Jesse Helms worked to keep Britt off the federal bench. A quarter of a century later, it was Judge W. Earl Britt's time to get even.

Martens did his homework well, though he also abandoned moral principles in the process by seeking the one judge in North Carolina who should not be on our case.

In ordering us to his jurisdiction and venue, however, it was Judge Britt who violated federal law and the Constitution. He had no lawful authority to rule in the case in the Eastern District or Raleigh Division, as both jurisdiction and venue had already *attached* in the Charlotte Division of the Western District. Outside jurisdiction and venue of charge, a judge cannot rule. Doing so renders action invalid, or "null and void," as the Public Defender explained to David Freedman at the Raleigh hearing. This is a constitutional matter, one decided by The Supreme Court in *Johnson v. Zerbst*, 304 US 458.

"The judgment of conviction pronounced by a court without jurisdiction is void, and one imprisoned thereunder may obtain release by habeas corpus."

How did we end up in this mess? We were caught in the middle of someone else's drama. Being asked to work with the prosecutors and agents was repulsive. Being told to inflict their evil onto someone else in order to save my own hide was equally troublesome. If I refused, which was the right thing to do, I might spend the rest of my life in prison, and not see our children grow up or be there as their parent.

I felt like Ulysses in *The Odyssey* as he navigated between Scylla, the multi-headed sea monster, and Charybdis, the bottomless whirlpool. The game they played had one victor and outcome, which isn't a game at all; it is being handed a fate. What swayed my thinking was the cold realization that my fate was also my wife's. I could make one move, and for an instant, I could affect the outcome. I could negotiate Vernice's freedom by working with them, and our children would have at least one parent for now.

After lunch I returned to the interrogation room on the second floor. AUSA Martens wasted no time setting the stage for how the afternoon would go. I'd asked all the questions I would be permitted, he told me. The afternoon belonged to him. I was to talk about Sam Currin and Jeremy Jaynes and nothing else.

I started at the beginning, in 2002, when Currin first called on our offices in The Bahamas. During a short meeting, I explained the formal and legal aspects of our trusts. As a U.S. attorney, Sam explicitly understood the intricacies and ramifications of our policies and procedures and was impressed President Reagan's trust attorney, Hiram Martin, was a partner and board member of our firm.

The briefing with Sam was complete. It included IRS opinions confirming the validity and legality of our structures, Hiram's legal opinions, and independent reviews of law by accounting and trust organizations. When I mentioned the IRS opinions, Schiller rifled through his file and brought out a copy of the same from my requests to his agency. This should have ended things then and there, but I was told to keep talking.

Sam called within two weeks, asking to return with a Colorado tax attorney. This visit was short but active. He claimed his client, Jeremy Jaynes, was voted 'young businessman of the year' in the Raleigh area and amassed his fortune of $20 plus million in Internet advertising.

When I said the number "$20 plus million," everyone in the room grabbed a pen and started writing. I immediately regretted saying that because we never saw Jaynes' proof, either from him or Sam. It was not uncommon for potential clients to initially exaggerate their wealth.

Sam described Jaynes' advertising activities as "travel and leisure," and "natural pharma," where his company made a fee for sales, collected gross receipts, and sent the residual to the client.

Jaynes joined us at some point during the meeting. He gestured toward the bay saying, "You see the harbor over there full of cruise ships? Our advertising filled over half of those berths. We use fax, printed mailers, and Internet advertising all together. It's very effective."

On the "natural pharma," Jaynes explained it included Viagra-like products, vitamins and supplements, which he said were booming sectors of Internet growth.

The company reportedly managed the payments, almost exclusively by credit card. The banks, he said, were a major problem for his company, as they not only took high transaction fees, but also withheld a large percentage of the gross payment against potential charge-backs on which they earned interest, but paid nothing to him or his clients. The charge-back withholding tied up money and restricted his growth. He wanted to make a major change.

Sam then broached the subject of his real interest, which was a banking license so the company could process charges through a related institution, reduce the unnecessary withholdings, and earn the fees instead of the large banks. Sam intended to be a part of the bank and assured me all those concerned were legitimate.

It was an interesting plan, and one that intrigued me. I was a member of The Bahamian Government's E-Commerce Committee and helped write their plan. Clearing banks were definitely obstacles to growth in Internet-related business activity. Sam knew I started a bank in the Far East some years before as well and recommended to Jeremy I assist in establishing theirs.

A meeting was arranged for them with the principals of KPMG, the largest accounting firm in Nassau, and with the Deputy Director of the Central Bank of The Bahamas, Mr. Kevin Higgins, who was a well-known author on international banking and advisor to governments and central banks.

KPMG wanted huge fees to research the issue. Mr. Higgins was quite frank, however, and advised us that The Bahamas would not issue a banking license to anyone unless first licensed in another country. Researching The Bahamas as a potential *situs* for that first license would be wasted money. Mr. Higgins understood the goal of the bank, a clearinghouse for Internet charges, and suggested we meet with and ask Visa-Latin America in Miami to recommend the jurisdiction. "Get your approval on the front end," he advised.

Seventy-three percent of all credit card business worldwide went through Visa at that time, so it appeared to be the obvious first stop. A meeting was arranged in Miami. Sam and I met with their executives as suggested by Mr. Higgins. Visa was keen on the idea, and suggested the relatively new banking jurisdiction of St. Lucia. We were assured of approval for credit card processing once the bank was licensed.

Meanwhile, through Sam's law firm, we incorporated companies for his client's Internet advertising business. One was established for each region of the world. We also established a trust structure for Mr. Jaynes to be the beneficiary of future income.

One of my partners in our trust company was a prominent St. Lucian. He agreed to assist in establishing a bank there. The next step was to meet with the regulators in St. Lucia. This too went smoothly. Accountants and attorneys were hired, and Saint Lucia's Prime Minister, Dr. Kenny Anthony, met with our group to encourage the process.

Other than a brief meeting in North Carolina where I was introduced to Jaynes' Canadian partner, I never heard from him more than twice again. All communication went through Sam Currin's law firm.

In the early summer of 2004, however, we began receiving lawsuits from a network of U.S. attorneys claiming our corporate management firm, Sterling ACS, Ltd., was a "fax-blaster" and sent unsolicited advertisements, an alleged violation of a state law in the U.S. The claim was untrue. Our firm never participated in such an advertising scheme, knew of, or authorized one.

We soon learned that the fuss was over a stock advertising promotion done by Jeremy Jaynes, using fax and Internet. He registered a stock promotion website using our company's name and contact information, without my permission or knowledge.

Additionally, stock promotion was not one of the approved activities under our trust arrangement, nor was one ever discussed, so we demanded Sam Currin immediately provide source of funds information on transfers wired to our trust company. Any funds related to stock promotion would be removed from trust control. Sam was informed that failure to provide this information would force us to resign as trustees and have him move his business elsewhere.

When the third request went unanswered, I filed a Suspicious Activity Report with the Central Bank. It stated the client refused to give the source of funds and was ordered to move his business. The report made no allegations of illegal conduct, as we knew no further details of activities other than information Jaynes initially supplied during his visit with Currin. However, the "fax-blaster" episode and the resultant allegations made by short-sellers against the firm gave us reason to question the real nature and methods of Jaynes' business and Currin, its agent. We gave them the benefit of the doubt, but made the necessary decision to terminate ourselves as trustees.

Throughout my story, agents and attorneys interrupted, suggesting this or that activity may have occurred, all in a transparent effort to create an illegality that never happened. Throughout my denials they made notes, false assurances. I found this disturbing.

If things were so certain for them, why did they look so desperate to have me confess?

"Something, anything," Martens had said.

Finally, FBI Agent Curran, who still didn't comprehend the made-up charges were simply to hold us as witnesses, said, "Surely you have done *something* wrong. Tell us about that."

By the time I finished describing the entire relationship with Currin, the day was gone. They learned no crime occurred and one couldn't be contrived out of anything said or done. To my knowledge, then as now, our firm and its agents never committed any crime, knowingly or otherwise. At the end of that day and for those that followed, I don't think these men cared about knowing what really happened. They came to ultimately tell me what they expected me to say, and hear it parroted. The truth was of no interest to them.

The sight of the portly deputy running them out of the interrogation room was a welcome one. It was once again "feeding" time in the Mecklenburg County Jail, and not even these FBI, IRS, and DOJ boys had the juice to override closing time.

I rode upstairs with the deputy in silence. Even on starvation rations, I could not muster an appetite that night. My body was covered with different dirt. I showered instead of eating. The metal bunk may as well have been a feather bed that night. I escaped misery in a deep sleep, wishing it all gone tomorrow.

CHAPTER 16

ANOTHER VISIT FROM THE FEDS

"Government is prohibited by the Sixth Amendment from deliberately eliciting incriminating evidence from accused after he has been indicted and in absence of his counsel."

United States v. Arnold, 106 F.3d 37 (3ʳᵈ Cir. 1997)

May 17, 2006 – Western District of North Carolina

Martens, Curran, and Schiller came again the morning of May 17, unannounced. I requested the Non-Attribution Agreement David promised would be sent April 27 and a copy of their *memorialized* agreement before sitting down. My wife was still in jail, though they promised her "immediate" release in exchange for the cooperation already given.

AUSA Martens did the shuffle of papers, and asked everyone around the table if they had copies of the agreements. David Freedman poked his head in for a minute between doing "something important" elsewhere in the jail. He and the prosecutor did the, "Oh, I thought you had given them to him" gag.

My brother, Jim, left almost daily messages with David to get us copies of these agreements. He had done so because I bothered Jim almost daily saying Freedman had not provided the agreements to me. I did so because David did not answer my letters or make it possible for me to speak to him by phone.

David left the interrogation room, once again, in spite of my telling him to stay. He took flight the moment Martens raised the issue of adding a money-laundering charge, claiming it would add "credibility" to me as a witness. This charge with its bogus reasoning violated both agreements we had made.

In a way, these illegal custodial interrogation sessions were a blessing. They allowed me to prove what happened from attorney/client correspondence rather than my journal alone. David was not present during these interrogations and would not take my calls, so I wrote him to complain about what happened in his absence. Those letters provide event records, which no one has ever been able to dispute. None present can be sure that another might refuse to lie under oath, if the matter were before a court. David Freedman cannot dispute the letters' content, as he made no rebuttal or offered a separate account at the time, either to me or to my file. Lacking such is an acceptance of my account. Instead, he claimed to subsequent counsel and the North Carolina State Bar that my correspondences did not exist until Judge Art Strickland's investigation some years later proved otherwise. One such record, from the May 19 meeting in 2006, said:

Their basic offer was that if I cooperated they stopped 'cold' at the items listed in their indictment. That was my inducement, and I accepted it.

But they're changing the game on me. Their inducement to 'stop the clock' was my reason, but Wednesday, they circumvented that inducement, reneged on our deal, and suggested on 3 occasions that they would want me to plead guilty to 'money-laundering', a charge not on their indictment and certainly not contemplated by me after our basic deal had been struck.

That's not stopping the clock. That's having your cake and eating it too. A deal is a deal. I agreed to help them and have kept my word. They promised to 'stop' where they were. They're now attempting to breach that understanding through the 'not so veiled' threat of many more years.

I need for you to aggressively stop this tactic now.

Howell W. Woltz

David claimed to Jim he did not receive this letter, though the copy from which I quote, came from his own files on order of the N.C. State Bar. From that point forward, as a precaution, I sent my letters to Jim's office for mailing to David so he couldn't irrefutably claim he did not receive them.

Having no response from the May 19 letter, I sent another to Jim's office to forward to David. His assistant, Kelly Kiser, not only mailed David the original, she scanned and e-mailed or faxed my handwritten copy as soon as she received it, then typed and sent another copy to him. These records have proven invaluable. On May 26, 2006, I wrote:

Dear David,

As of today, your office telephone is still a "restricted number." My 80-year-old mother has figured this out, David. All someone had to do is call 1-800-844-6591. I feel isolated enough in here without my attorney denying access. I'm not interested in continuing working with you if I have no way to contact you.

If you can't, or won't take care of this, please send back the retainer minus whatever time has been spent and we'll move on.

These guys are already changing the game on me, but I've had no possibility to talk to you about it. Another week plus has drifted by and I've heard from no one.

Have you called them on this money-laundering charge they're trying to sneak in after saying all had "stopped"? I'm having trouble understanding why you didn't jump up and scream when they said it.

What's next? What other charges will you let them add?

I need a lot more aggressive assistance than that. I can sit there and let them ride rip-shod over me with a court appointed lawyer. For the fee you've been paid, I need someone fighting for me.

So far, we have:

1. *IRS Charges. IRS Agent Scott Schiller admitted on the afternoon of our first meeting that we had not broken any IRS laws. He flatly stated that in front of the whole room. This leaves conspiracy. How can I "conspire" to not break the law? That's nonsense and he admitted it.*

2. *The "perjury" and "obstruction" charges were the result of testimony solicited by the U.S. Attorney's Office from the (confessed) criminals that are the defendants in case CV04-1512* **[NOTE: This was 2004 case,** *United States v. J. Vernon Abernethy, CPA,* **in the U.S. District Court of New Jersey, where Abernethy had given testimony in direct conflict with that he gave the grand jury in our case].** *The government "exchanged" this false testimony for an agreement not to file criminal charges against Abernethy, who cost our clients millions of dollars. His testimony in New Jersey, which I asked you to discuss with Marty Russo* **[our company attorney in New York]** *five weeks ago, shows Abernethy changing this story 3 times. Marty's cross-examination destroyed his story. I'm going to assume you haven't followed up with Marty. We can destroy this crook on the stand with his own testimony from depositions and testimony he's given.*

3. *The now-proposed "money-laundering" plea. The Fourth Circuit Court of Appeals has ruled that the mere "consideration" of a plea deal by government can be deemed acceptance.*

4. *The government more than "considered" our arrangement, they agreed to the deal. "You cooperate, Mr. Woltz, and this stops here!"* **[Those were AUSA Martens exact words on April 27th, 2006]**

5. *I've cooperated, they've now changed the deal. I don't appreciate being treated like a fool by these people. I need for you to either aggressively point out these weaknesses to them to get a better deal, or tell them to go to Hell and we fight them.*

If we are to continue, I need some time with you other than in front of the Feds to plan a new bond hearing where we mount a vigorous case. We also need to develop a proactive strategy for dealing with the government on this plea arrangement.

They've toyed with us now for 6 weeks. I've lived up to all my commitments. They've kept none. Per Doug Curran [the FBI Agent], *I'm the most "forthright and honest witness in [his] career." He, Martens & Meyers have all lied to me.... At some point, we need to call them on their equity issues. We may need to reconsider our strategy if they continue the dishonesty.*

Regards,

Howell

The most bizarre aspect of this attempt to add a money laundering *conspiracy*, in retrospect, is that the funds being discussed were never charged as being criminally derived. One can't "knowingly launder proceeds of crime" when there has yet to be any charge of criminal origin or knowledge of any crime. All of the funds in question came to our trust firm from licensed U.S. regulated brokerage houses and law firms which had the responsibility as sender, under law, to do due diligence on their origin. We did not know what transpired before those funds came to us and could not have known. If criminal stock activity was being conducted, the trading firms and brokers in the United States were the wrong doers, not us. We received the wires from those licensed financial institutions and law firms without further information, and ultimately turned away Sam Currin's business when he failed to provide the original source of those funds once suspicions were raised.

What Martens was doing to me was akin to sending a man to prison for *fencing* stolen goods, without ever claiming anything stolen. If the goods themselves were not stolen, how could the person who sold them be guilty of "knowingly" fencing stolen goods? It's like forcing someone to plead guilty to murder without anyone dying.

By May of 2006, all of the original, fabricated charges were falling apart (and were eventually dismissed), with the exception of the alleged "conspiracy." Agent Schiller admitted at our first meeting this charge was a hoax, and I forwarded that information to Freedman by letter. Unless Attorney Rick Graves or I pled guilty to something that never happened, it was highly unlikely that one remaining charge could stand as well.

Martens clearly realized he needed to fabricate something else against me, if I were to be held much longer, as the original slate was falling apart. I refused to sign a guilty plea, or Plea Agreement as it is known, so I was still free to go to trial, and his charges could not stand the least scrutiny or adversarial process. His Non-Affinity Agreement also stated he could not add any more charges in exchange for the assistance I already provided. Nonetheless, he fabricated the money laundering *conspiracy* in violation of that agreement, and asked me to plead guilty to it on May 17, knowing my attorney was AWOL, and he was, therefore, free to violate federal law. May 17 was the thirtieth day since our arrest and also the last day he could legally add a new charge under the thirty-day rule of 18 U.S.C. §3161(b), making his actions all the more cunning. I was unaware of the time limitations back then, but as an attorney for government, Martens was.

Neither David Freedman nor AUSA Martens gave me their "memorialized notes" or a copy of their Non-Attribution Agreement precluding such a charge. Martens decided to breach those agreements when the original charges fell apart. Both Martens and Freedman clearly expected me to agree to plead guilty without a fight, which is exactly what most people do. Ninety-five percent of cases are now settled in that fashion, though the Sixth Amendment still requires all criminal cases to be tried before a jury.

Martens also knew I was upset with David. I suppose he knew if I fired David and got a real attorney, government might have a formidable opponent and a severe problem, possibly a suit for false charges and imprisonment. He came that day with the intent of forcing me to "voluntarily" accept the charge in the absence of my lawyer, but I refused to do so.

After threats did not work, he offered a carrot. He asked, "What do you want?" I didn't know whether he was getting ready to attempt to bribe me or make another 'deal,' but all I wanted was to get Martens and our case before an honest judge.

"I want Judge Graham Mullen [Chief Judge of the Western District and Charlotte Division] to hear the case *here*. I don't want

Judge Britt to hear it down in Raleigh. That's not right." Judge Mullen, according to other prisoners with experience, was known for fair proceedings, and not particularly tolerant of certain prosecutorial play.

Martens flushed and his lips tightened. He said very slowly and angrily, "Judge Graham Mullen will *never* hear *this* case."

At the end of this session, something very strange happened. FBI Agent Doug Curran stayed behind as the others left the interrogation room. Hours of my refutations and Agent Schiller's own admissions of fabricating the case against me appeared to have had an effect on him.

Agent Curran reached out, shook my hand, and said, "Mr. Woltz, I just want to apologize for what we have done to you and your family. I will not be staying on this case, and you will not be seeing me anymore."

AUSA Martens saw this and re-opened the door.

"Come on Curran," he said angrily. "We have to go."

Curran paid him no attention other than to nod in Martens' direction and add, "I hope you understand that is all I can say right now," and with that, he followed Martens out, leaving me briefly in thought until the guard arrived.

True to his word, that was the last meeting he attended. IRS agent, David "Scott" Schiller, admitted we "broke no law" on April 27. By May 19, the FBI agent in charge was apologizing for "what we've done to you and your family," and quit the case. It seemed impossible for the sham prosecution to continue, not if any of them respected the law or themselves.

I thought back to the night in Nassau when Sam Currin nearly cried, telling us how he feared meeting his Maker without first making apologies, on his knees, to his victims of similar persecution. Was young Martens Sam Currin of old?

CHAPTER 17

FEDERAL JUDGE RAPS SENTENCING GUIDELINES

Chief Judge Graham C. Mullen to Western District U.S. Attorney and Assistants:

"Your office is perceived as acting like arrogant bullies who over-indict, always believe snitches, threaten defendants who seek release on bond, always seek to get the max and go for the jugular....I can no longer stomach the gross injustices I am required to announce."

May 29, 2006 – Western District of North Carolina

A buzz shot through the pod when the *Charlotte Observer* hit that day. The front-page article blared "Federal Judge Raps Sentencing Guidelines," quoting Graham C. Mullen, Chief District Judge of the Western District of North Carolina. He berated the Western District Office of the U.S. Attorney and its minions. The quote came from his speech to the U.S. Attorneys at their conference in Boone, NC.

The article also said, "Mullen surprised many in the legal community by announcing *he would no longer accept most plea agreements.*

He said the agreements, which forced criminal suspects to give up their rights to appeal, were *unconscionable.*" It was now clear why AUSA Martens so forcefully stated on May 19 Judge Mullen would *never* hear *my* case. Martens had done precisely what Judge Mullen banned and could not go before him without consequence.

Judge Mullen's speech in 2003 was during the tenure of Western District U.S. Attorney Robert J. Conrad, Jr., who was moved to the Eastern District-Raleigh Division shortly after Judge Mullen accused his office of these unconstitutional practices. By coincidence, the position he assumed was once held by my co-defendant, Sam Currin. Robert J. Conrad, Jr. followed Sam as U.S. Attorney in Judge W. Earl Britt's court in Raleigh.

It was rumored that month in Mecklenburg that U.S. Attorney Robert Conrad, Jr., recently appointed Federal District Court Judge by President George Bush, would be returning to Charlotte to take Judge Mullen's place as Chief of the Western District.

I copied the entire article in my journal for further study, as I could not immediately process all the information.

There was another peeling of the onion. Martens broke federal law to keep us out of Judge Mullens' court. That was now clear, as was his reason for it. The Public Defender pointed out to David Freedman in Raleigh that I could not be taken to Britt's venue for bond revocation or for any other adjudication. His court had no jurisdiction in the case in a district foreign to that of charge. Seeking bond revocation there was a federal crime on Martens' part and Britt's agreement to hear the case in his district violated my rights under the Fifth and Sixth Amendments.

18 U.S.C. §3145(a)(1) **Review of a Release Order** states: "the attorney for the Government may file, *with the court having original jurisdiction over the offense,* a motion for revocation of the order or amendment of the conditions of release."

The only court with "original jurisdiction" was the Charlotte Division of the Western District of North Carolina. The only District Court Judge in that Division with the authority to override Magistrate

Judge Keesler's release order was Chief Judge Graham C. Mullen, the man Martens swore to keep from hearing it.

By his own admission, Martens orchestrated the Western District Clerk of Court's, "Johnsy", to re-assign the case to a foreign judge and venue. By taking us to Raleigh and Judge Britt, Martens was keeping the case out of Judge Mullen's sight until former Western District U.S. Attorney Robert Conrad, Jr., returned to take Judge Mullens' place and things could go back to *normal*.

"Normal," according to the article, included unconstitutional tactics and plea agreements unlawfully coerced by then U.S. Attorney Robert Conrad, Jr. and his assistants. It seemed unlikely that putting a black robe on Conrad would change his nature or improve his morals and judicial practices. I had to get us out of Britt's court in Raleigh and back to Charlotte in front of Judge Graham C. Mullen before any changes took place.

This was not going to be easy. By letter, I instructed Freedman to challenge the jurisdiction and venue violations, file charges of prosecutorial misconduct against Martens, and then file a complaint against Judge Britt for participating in it. Judge Mullen needed to know what was being done behind his back, and we needed to do it before Conrad took over. There was little chance of "Judge" Conrad enforcing laws he so wantonly disregarded in Judge Mullen's estimation. I wrote letter after letter to Freedman without response. The few times he came to see me, he claimed to be "looking into it."

CHAPTER 18

THE LONG HAUL

"If a defendant is not brought to trial within the time limit required by section 3161(c) [seventy days] as extended by section 3161(h) [excludable delays], the information or indictment shall be dismissed on motion of the defendant. Failure of the defendant to move for dismissal prior to trial or entry of a plea of guilty or nolo contendere shall constitute a waiver of the right to dismissal under this section." 18 U.S.C. §3162(a)(2)

June 29, 2006 – Western District of North Carolina

My letter of instructions to Freedman May 7, 2006, the third week after arrest, stated:

"I don't want to allow any motions for extension, or <u>any</u> motions that cause delay. My life and livelihood are on hold for charges that are false. Please be prepared to move for dismissal after 70 days (June 29th) as allowed under 18 U.S.C. §3161, et seq."

Howell W. Woltz, TEP

Had David or any other attorney I later hired, filed this Motion to Dismiss Indictment on June 29, 2006, or any day thereafter, my story would have ended, according to the statute. Though each of my attorneys was so ordered, not one complied.

The law above requires that charges against a defendant not tried within seventy days *"shall be dismissed on motion of the defendant."* The word "shall" is positive legal language, meaning the court does not have a choice. It must dismiss the entire indictment if the defendant files for it.

Seventy days is the legal time limit for a trial to begin under the Sixth Amendment and Speedy Trial Act. It can only be extended by what are known as "excludable delays." This is a short list of reasons used to stop the speedy trial clock. There are only seven of them, and they are listed under §3161(h) of The Speedy Trial Act, which is the law I cited to David Freedman in the letter sent on May 7.

There were no such excludable delays cited in the case or in continuance motions, meaning the speedy trial clock never stopped. Under the Professional Code of Conduct, an attorney does not have any choice but to follow his or her client's lawful instructions. The relationship between an attorney and a client is one of *principal and agent*, not one of *guardian and ward*. An attorney is required under the Professional Code to zealously defend his or her clients, and must follow their instructions as to how to proceed in a case. Not doing so in matters such as proving government and a federal judge broke the law is a crime in itself and also in violation of the Professional Code of Conduct. Failure to file a simple motion, which would, by law, set the client free, is malpractice. The client should not have to ask a competent attorney to do so, but once the client has, the attorney can either comply or resign from the case.

As spring turned to summer and weeks became months, it became clear that David Freedman did not file the Motion to Dismiss as ordered. I could not occupy my time with case journals knowing absolutely nothing was happening. I was bored. There were only so many hours I could meditate and very little of value to read in the murderer's pod.

One day a young man asked if I would review his case.

"Why did you choose me?"

"White man with glasses. A white man wearing glasses always knows something about the law."

While I could not agree with his logic, I agreed to read his case file. The young man, just out of the military, was arrested without probable cause. He and his car were searched without a warrant. After finding a small amount of marijuana in his pocket, the police arrested him. They added a charge for a shotgun found in his grandmother's home (that belonged to his dead grandfather), and another for possession of a weapon by a drug user for the same gun. He faced five years mandatory for the gun charge alone. The indictment revealed government misconduct and numerous violations of constitutional rights, but his attorney was unwilling to challenge the prosecutor. After arraignment, the lawyer said the young man should have pled guilty, and that was the last he was seen.

Another man I met in Pod 6800, Michael Sherrill, was accused of more murders than Jack the Ripper. The longer he refused to plead guilty, the more "cold cases" the local prosecutor added. Michael had been in the murderer's pod for years, though government was required to try him within seventy days. He is now on death row in Central Prison in Raleigh. I received a letter from him in January, 2013 stating the DNA evidence government claimed to have at his first trial could not be produced. The state said it had, "gone missing." Michael wrote:

"But as slow as these people go, Woltz, I will probably die of old age before I get this straightened out. Took 3 years to get them to look at the DNA evidence again! But as you and I know, the truth doesn't have to set you free in N.C. But at least I got hope again!"

Michael loaned books to me and was my spades partner when they let us out for a few hours at night. I knew him better than anyone. He was a loner with a record from his younger days, but he turned his life around and did not have so much as a speeding ticket in eighteen years when we met. Michael knew the system from having been in prison in his youth, and used to tell me, "Never talk about your case or give the snitches any information to make up a story about you. All they want is to get a time-cut in their own sentence. If you have to talk to them, never tell them the truth." Although I was known as the "jailhouse lawyer" and closest to him, Michael never told me about his case, except that he was innocent of the charges and would one day prove it.

Fascinated by his letter, I contacted his investigator to learn more, with Michael's permission. Mike's cases are from 1984. The Fed-Ex contractor for whom Michael worked tracked packages thereby monitoring his time and location. They were able to get these records and prove he was not in the states where all but two of the cold cases were charged. Federal money is made available to help local governments solve old cases; this makes conditions ripe for local officials to seek false testimony in hopes of closing them (and getting the money) while commuting sentences of jailhouse informants. Two of the cases were from Michael's hometown of Gastonia, NC; the only two that could not be eliminated by the tracking records.

The State gave Michael a death sentence on the first charge and has yet to try him on the second. I find it highly unlikely he ever gave anyone information or discussed his case as the State and its jailhouse informant claims.

With the alleged DNA evidence "gone missing," all the prosecutor has is a compensated snitch and the testimony of Michael's ex-girlfriend, government's first suspect in the murder until she agreed to testify against Michael in exchange for immunity. This trial is scheduled later this year, three decades after the alleged crime. There is no justice in this, and Michael has now lost ten years of his life, and may lose it altogether, if the State of North Carolina has its way.

These cases came at me one after another. All but a few had two common threads, 1) government/prosecutorial/judicial misconduct to get a conviction, and 2) attorneys unwilling to zealously defend their clients or force government and courts to follow the law.

Some of the men in the murderers' pod belonged behind bars. Most of them, the *real* criminals, however, were also the snitches, working their sentences away by helping government convict other men. The others, like Michael Sherrill, I suspected were innocent. Many of government's best snitches had, by their own admission, committed heinous crimes and were truly dangerous people.

In my experience, those who *should* be in prison are the ones generally working their way to freedom by putting those who *don't* belong, in prison. The system is working backwards. It appears to be driven by convictions rather than justice, as former U.S. Attorney Sam Currin professed years before.

Jail is a small place. Truly evil men and their stories are unavoidable, but many of the worst seemed to disappear. They got bond and returned to the streets, a wrongful and public danger, to create more cases for government. The FBI did the same in the case of Whitey Bulger in Boston, Massachusetts. As long as Whitey worked for them, he murdered, but was protected by his FBI handlers. Such men become de facto government agents, and know they can literally get away with murder, as long as they are feeding the prosecutors and agents more defendants as Whitey Bulger did.

While the Bulger case may be an extreme example, that scheme is at work to some extent in every jail and prison I visited across the nation.

Most of the men in the murderer's pod did not belong in that violent place, and the more I heard and saw, the more shocked I became. I looked at cases every day and saw that mine was anything but unique. The same problems repeated, indicating our system of justice was rendered a system of injustices. The instituted corruption appears to be readily accepted by those involved, and incentives for maintaining the *status quo* are firmly in place. Prosecutors thrive and prosper only on convictions, and attorneys make a good livelihood by staying out of their way. It works for everyone except the system's victims: American citizens charged with a crime.

As for those men who did *something*, many were subjected to illegal searches and seizures, warrantless arrests, over-indictment, unlawful detention and other bizarre and unconstitutional treatments. I began learning about the law, motivated more by disgust and less by desire.

Although it is a constitutional right to have access to court and law when detained, not one of my requests to visit the jail's law library was granted. A deputy finally told me to quit turning them in. He said, "We've been told by the prosecutor to never let you see the inside of the jail's law library, Woltz, so you're wasting your time turning in these requests."

When I later filed a lawsuit against the sheriff for this denial, the local federal court, in its dismissal of the suit, explained since North Carolina has a *legal aid service*, the jail does not have to comply with the Sixth Amendment requirement. My evidence in the lawsuit was the denial itself of legal aid services, but the clerk of court ("Johnsy") did not file my evidence and attachments, proving the claim. I sent Art a copy of it, including the evidence. Those documents were not on PACER, the public's access to court records. The Clerk refused to file it, though it was attached to the lawsuit. That was not an accident, and having no access to PACER, I would never have known what was done, absent Art Strickland watching the case.

I appealed the ruling to the Fourth Circuit, which dismissed it without meaningful review or reason. I then appealed to the Supreme Court, which denied *certiorari*, refusing to hear it. I can only surmise from this experience that the courts in general do not want detained citizens to have access to law, despite the Sixth Amendment requiring it. The net result is for the accused to be held in dangerous, crowded conditions, without access, until he or she gives up and agrees to plead guilty, having no other recourse.

That accurately summarizes the system of justice I have witnessed and experienced. It is easier for attorneys to go along with this corruption than fight powerful prosecutors. The attorneys make much the same money without expending the effort to research their clients' cases or go to trial, and the number of clients an attorney can handle is nearly without limit, as little if any time is spent on their defense. It became clear: My mission was to help those being abused and ignored by those whose job it was to defend them.

The first success in getting someone freed was so intoxicating I knew helping these men was my niche for as long as the nightmare continued. J.R. (Fitzgerald) Stephenson, had been illegally held by the State of North Carolina for twenty-one months when I met him in the murderer's pod. It took about fifteen minutes to see that the charge against him was impossible. J.R. was a 6 ' 6" giant, weighing 275 pounds, with hardly an ounce of fat on his body. He also had a deformity from a terrible car wreck. His neck was not set properly and was larger than my waist after a short time on the Mecklenburg diet. The deformity was impossible to go unnoticed.

When I read the police report, however, the victims described the robber as "a small black man, 5 foot 10 inch, clean-shaven, weighing approximately 165 pounds." The report further described him as having "no distinguishing marks or features."

When people saw J.R. Stephenson, their jaws dropped. He was that big, and the neck deformity was so obvious that the fellows sometimes called him "turkey-neck" behind his back. He had a beard in his mug shot the night of the arrest, though the thief from the same night was "clean-shaven."

I did not know exactly what to do since I was banned from the law library, but one of the law books sent by my sister-in-law, Jill, mentioned an old statute known as the "Ku Klux Klan Act" passed in 1871. The statute, 42 U.S.C.§1983, was designed to allow blacks in the post-Civil War south to seek justice directly with federal courts when their rights were violated under color or law by state officials.

A preacher in pod 6800 offered to investigate the case upon his release. He found there was no "confidential informant" in J.R.'s case, as claimed. Adam 1 (the cop) told Adam 2 (the other cop) as they drove down the street, "Let's get that big guy." It was a case of wrong place and time.

The police and prosecutor decided to let J.R. sit in jail until he agreed to say that he did it, no matter how many years it took and despite all evidence proving he was not the man. They knew eventually he would do so, just to get out of the murderer's pod. About the identical time, I became certain that AUSA Matthew Martens and Judge Britt were doing the same thing to my wife and me.

I filed a federal lawsuit against the two police officers for violating J.R.'s constitutional rights, and added their chief, for knowingly allowing their criminal conduct.

We sued them for $950,000. All charges were immediately dropped against J.R., and he was set free. I received a thank-you note for helping. It described his plan to open "J.R.'s Kountry Kitchen" with the money, if they ever paid him, and included a hand-written menu.

That was my first "win," and it felt good. The cases came in rapid succession after that.

Not *everyone* in the murderer's pod was innocent, and I don't wish to convey that, but the percentage of wrongfully incarcerated would shock any reviewer who took the time to examine their cases. Why weren't the lawyers doing something about it? I guessed for the same reasons mine wasn't.

Noe Moreno came forward after J.R.'s release. He and his brother were in a head-on collision one night. Noe's brother was driving the car, and their best friend was killed in the back seat.

Both brothers were unconscious when EMS arrived. The top of the car was cut off to extract their bodies. The attendant police, EMS medics, doctors, and every person in the chain correctly identified Noe's brother as the driver. He was extracted from the driver's seat by the medics and upon regaining consciousness at the hospital, affirmed his role as driver. The following day, however, the detective notes stated, "after a call from my sergeant" he changed the report to state Noe Moreno was driver instead of his brother.

Noe had a DWI on his record. The prosecutor decided it would be far easier to get a manslaughter conviction against him rather than his brother. The police changed their report to comply with the prosecutor, without question, knowing this to be contrary to their own reports.

Despite this evidence, the local prosecutor, Peter S. Gilchrist III, charged Noe with manslaughter. His brother was threatened with first degree murder if Noe refused to say he was the driver and plead guilty to the false charge of manslaughter.

Noe's court-appointed lawyer refused to address the issue or to question the prosecutor and police on these discrepancies or their misconduct. I wrote him several letters on Noe's behalf, as he did not speak English, but the attorney never responded. I prepared another suit against the police, but was pulled out of the pod before its filing.

I was temporarily shipped out on what is known as *diesel therapy,* where a prisoner is moved unnecessarily from jail to jail. The guards learned what I was doing from a pod snitch, or so was reported, and I was removed to prevent filing the suit.

When I was taken, Noe took the false charge and agreed to a sentence by plea agreement to protect his brother. He was on his way to prison for seven years on a crime he never committed when I last heard of him.

This type of conduct is criminal and merely serves to enhance the career of the prosecutor. Outcome over justice, is the common approach now used. In just a few months, what I witnessed changed me forever. I understood why few of these men in jail had any respect for the law. Government had become the lawbreaker.

The question, "Why me?" was answered with, "You're supposed to do something about it."

CHAPTER 19

ANOTHER DECEPTION

"The trial of any person described in subsection (a)
(1) or (a)(2) ["high risk"] shall commence not later than
ninety days following the beginning of such continuous
detention or designation of high risk by the attorney for the
Government. Failure to commence trial shall result in the
*automatic review by the court of the conditions of release.
No detainee, as defined in subsection (a), shall be held in
custody pending trial after the expiration of such ninety-day
period required for the commencement of his trial.*"

18 U.S.C. §§3164(b) & (c)

July 27, 2006 – Western District of North Carolina

My final meeting with AUSA Matthew Martens came on July 27, again, without notice. Law required us to have been tried one month before. The above law further demanded that if for any reason we had not been tried, we must be released under that statute's "automatic review" provision "after the expiration of such ninety-day period." The ninetieth day was July 19. Our imprisonment thereafter was in violation of federal law and I was not legally supposed to be in jail the day they came.

David Freedman not only showed up for this final meeting with the prosecutor, he stayed the whole time. This never before had happened. AUSA Martens still needed a claim that I had been in a *conspiracy* to violate a law. He knew without the leverage of false imprisonment and my wife as a hostage that would not happen. He and his Eastern District Judge kept us incarcerated in violation of federal law, effectively denying us legal assistance and the opportunity to challenge their wrongdoing.

If Martens could coerce the claim that we were in a "conspiracy", then he had to prove nothing. One little lie on my part, and Currin, Jaynes and whoever Martens wanted to add, all went to jail or had to give up their money. It was a shakedown.

But at that point, no crime had been charged against the others for any activity that related to us, our company, Vernice or me. *Conspiracy* was their effective strategy and shortcut, untrue as it was.

The unannounced visit from AUSA Martens on July 27, 2006, therefore, was no mere social call. David Freedman was with him because they knew I had reached my limit, along with Doug Curran's replacement from the FBI, but I was done with all of them.

The meeting was brief and to the point. If I did not agree to lie under oath and say Sam Currin's clients broke the law, and say I knew they did so, AUSA Martens and the FBI *"would be on my doorstep for the rest of my life, indicting me until they made 'something stick'."* Martens left it up to me to invent these imaginary meetings and create a story. Each time I repeated that there were no such meetings and he knew it, he replied, "Then you must *remember* them."

Further, AUSA Martens said I had to agree to lie about Attorney Rick Graves, and claim he and I were also in a conspiracy to defraud the U.S. Government. That would have to be invented as well, as I had never been alone with Rick Graves and only recalled meeting him on a couple of occasions. Their recordings of the meetings with their undercover con men proved AUSA Martens' charges were fabricated. Only by getting me to invent meetings and conversations, could he win these cases.

Fortunately, I don't have to remember what each said because I wrote David Freedman yet another letter detailing the conversation:

"Our willingness to cooperate…was based on their false commitments and promises to:

> *1. The immediate release of my wife who has now been held hostage since April 18, 2006.*
> *2. No new charges of any kind. Period.*
> *3. Our personal assets and those of our clients were said to be of no interest and you confirmed the government's representation that there would be no attempt at confiscation at our last meeting.*

WHERE WE ARE:

> • *My wife-months later- is still a hostage.*
> • *Only new charges are now being contemplated, as the original charges can't be substantiated.*
> • *The only document I've been allowed to see calls for seizure and confiscation of all assets; personal, or under any type of control, and a possible fine of $750,000.00.*

Of the plea they wanted me to accept, I wrote:
The plea I'm being recommended to sign is:

> *1. Only being considered for the sake of a contingent plea agreement for my wife as they've specifically stated that the two are tied together. I don't sign what they give me, she stays in jail. I'm amazed that such is legal, but am assuming that if it were not, you would have not only advised me of it, but taken action against them for doing it.*
> *2. The plea is a lie. I'm being pressured to sign a lie to get my hostage wife out of jail. That is the only reason there is even a conversation going on about it.*

3. *If I don't sign the plea, [AUSA] Martens said that he and the FBI would "be on my doorstep for the rest of my life, indicting me until they made 'something stick.' That's a pretty big stick to be threatened by when the bearer is the 'Justice' Dept. of the most powerful government on earth."*

The "lifetime of indictments" was a heavy weight to bear. They were threatening to hold my wife in jail for years, if I did not lie for them. I refused the deal and walked out of the room. The guard told me I could not leave until the men in the room told me I could.

I said, "Go fuck yourself."

I was immediately taken back to the murderer's pod, unafraid and determined. We would find a way to get before an honest judge and court.

CHAPTER 20

TERMINATION

*"A single error of counsel may constitute
ineffectiveness of counsel."*

Murray v. Carrier, 477 U.S. 478 (1986)

August 29, 2006 – Western District of North Carolina

After that meeting, I ordered a copy of the docket sheet in my case from the Clerk's office and had a friend search for the State Bar magazine cover story about David Freedman. I wanted to see if David filed the Motion for Dismissal or any of the other motions, as he claimed to have done and to see the State Bar magazine article to read how anyone determined he was "the best criminal defense lawyer in North Carolina." When I got the docket sheet, there was not a single entry on my behalf. David had lied to me for months.

The magazine cover he displayed the first day we met was not a publication of the State Bar. It was from *Superlawyers*, a magazine that sells its cover and writes friendly articles about attorneys for a fee, as promo materials for their practices. It was a hoax.

On August 29, I filed this letter with the Clerk of Court and copied David:

Dear David,

I have ordered and received a copy of the docket report on my case and see that there has been no activity on my behalf, period.

If the time has passed for filing the various motions requested, you need to notify your malpractice carrier.

Please immediately return the retainer, my files on this case including copies of all correspondence, and the cell phone that was mailed to you by Jim Woltz.

I will be seeking other counsel now.

Sincerely,

Howell W. Woltz

No money was ever returned, and David refused to turn over my files. He did, however, return the phone Jim had provided, one with a $500 pre-paid credit on the expensive jailhouse system. He elected to never answer it.

David came to see me three times the week after being fired, bringing offers of "deals" from Judge Britt, or so he claimed. I wrote a letter directly to Judge Britt challenging his lack of jurisdiction and the venue violations. My letter was a substitute for what David failed to do. No matter. The court was on notice, and I was seeking a dismissal of the indictment. In a fair court, that would have acted as a *pro se* motion requiring our immediate release under The Speedy Trial Act.

David brought the original handwritten letter I mailed Judge Britt. He said Britt promised that Martens would be forced to live by the original deal of April 27 if I would withdraw my letter-motions to the Court. That was *ex parte* and illegal, but the fact that David had the original Britt letter led me to believe he was telling the truth. Britt was again skirting the law. I refused the offer and filed copies of all of my letters to Britt and the FBI about the illegal conduct in the case. These are still of record as Items #88-94 on the Docket Sheet of Case No. 3:06-cr-074. I also told David Freedman to never come see me again.

CHAPTER 21

THE SEARCH FOR AN HONEST MAN

"An accused has a fundamental right to be represented by counsel of his own choice." *Powell v. Alabama,* **287 US 45, 77 L.Ed.158, 53 S.Ct. 55**

September 1, 2006 – Western District of North Carolina

T he Greek Cynic philosopher Diogenes, as the story goes, used to walk the streets, barefoot, carrying a lamp in broad daylight, seeking an honest man. Period biographers wrote he was looking for a 'human being,' but I admit preferring the moral lesson and legend to the more official account. By September of 2006 I too was looking for an honest man.

My task was much more difficult. Diogenes could crawl out from under the old washtub where he lived, and wander all of Asia Minor in his search, but I was stuck in the murderer's pod in Charlotte and could go nowhere. The honest man I sought must also have a law degree and be licensed to practice in the Great State of North Carolina.

The Mecklenburg County Jail provided no lists of attorneys or phone books, but I had no choice except to find another lawyer. We were three months beyond the date by which law required us to be tried, and two months beyond the date of our mandatory release.

The more I asked about attorneys, the more depressed I became. Some men in the murderer's pod had gone years without a visit or noticeable action from their lawyers.

One day, however, I heard the man from the next cell say something positive about an attorney he'd hired to replace his court appointed lawyer. That was a first. My neighbor's first attorney did exactly what David Freedman had done. He promised a firm deal was made with the prosecutor. If Antonio Smith *cooperated,* then they would let him go. He did, but was sentenced to sixteen years and eight months in prison.

Antonio said he found a young, aggressive, black attorney, Tolly A. Kennon III, who sought to overturn the sentence. Those in earshot bet attorney Kennon wouldn't last two years in Charlotte before they ruined or ran him out of town.

I wrote Mr. Kennon a note stating my attorney was terminated for lying, refusing to follow instructions, and not defending me. I wanted to fight the charges, but would not hire another attorney until I interviewed him. He came, and we arrived at a clear understanding; trial was my only objective. I could not take another Freedman.

Tolly Albert Kennon III was a big man, and he was on a mission to clean up the corruption. He was professional but friendly. I liked him immediately. He did not want my case unless I was serious about fighting it, which was refreshing. So too was his secondary concern about money, for it was I who finally brought up the matter of fees, and he let me set the price.

Yes, I liked Mr. Kennon. He was the honest lawyer I was seeking, and my spirits began to rise.

CHAPTER 22

THE PLOT THICKENS

"A lawyer shall not represent a private client in connection with a matter in which the lawyer participated personally and substantially as a public officer or employee, and no lawyer in a firm with which that lawyer is associated may knowingly undertake or continue in such representation."

Disciplinary Rule 9-101, *Avoiding Even the Appearance of Impropriety*, **Professional Code of Conduct for Attorneys**

October 1, 2006 – Western District to the Eastern District

Martens and Judge Britt didn't welcome the energetic Tolly Kennon. He came of record in the case on September 22, 2006. Nine days later, I was ordered to pack my belongings for another road trip to the Eastern District.

Vernice was downstairs to be packed out as well. We gave each other the usual questioning look. We wrote each other every day, expressing doubt, confusion, and a profound sense of isolation, but neither of us knew what was happening. I wasn't prepared to see her gaunt and defeated. I could tell by her appearance the experience was killing her.

I refused to leave without my legal papers, as they were taken and not returned the time before. After an extended argument, I was allowed to carry them. My wife, even in her frail condition, rose to the occasion and fought to keep her papers and files as well. We were put into the marshal's van, hands, feet, and waist, chain-bound. En route, in tears, she whispered, "How could you do it?"

I had no idea what she meant. "Do what?" I asked.

"Mr. Tisdale said you were going to tell lies about me for Martens, to get yourself free. They've been trying to get me to do that to you for months, but I've refused. I could never do that to you, Howell. How could you...?" she said, but trailed off into sobs.

"I could never do anything like that, Vernice! You know that."

"So you've never talked to them about that?" Her pained look lessened.

"On all that is sacred to me – on our two son – I swear it. The last time I saw Matthew Martens, he tried to force me to lie about Jaynes and Graves. If he couldn't get me to do that, how do you think he could talk me into telling lies about my own wife? I fired Freedman shortly after that. Don't you see what they are doing? They have no case against us, so they're trying to turn us against each other! Tisdale and Freedman are helping them. Unless one of us lies about the other, they can't convict us. We never committed a crime. The IRS agent admitted it!"

She broke into tears from happiness, rather than grief, and we gently put our heads together. For a brief moment, joy freed us, despite the chains.

I told her all that happened with David Freedman and about hiring Tolly Kennon. We pledged not to let these malevolent men, especially those in our own employ, succeed in driving a wedge between us.

Neither of us had any idea why we were being dragged to Raleigh, but Vernice made the decision to change attorneys, assuming Britt's court was our destination.

Our new strategy solidified. Relieved of our initial plea merchant attorneys, we would both work with Tolly and fight.

I was put in the Yellow Pod of The Wake County Jail on the fifth floor. There were the usual scuffles and shouting matches over the phones, but this was worse than the Blue Pod on my previous visit. Two rival gangs maneuvered for control and fights were frequent.

I tried to determine the number of men, but movement, scuffles and chaos disrupted the effort after sixty-three. The pod was designed to hold twenty-three.

The only piece of floor not taken was just outside the communal toilet, and each time the door opened, it slammed into my mat, making sleep nearly impossible. A third gang, one busted that afternoon, occupied the room beside it. Small packets of crack and powder cocaine were woven into their dreadlocks. Drugs were traded throughout the night to other prisoners for commissary and future food.

It was an unbelievable sight. With so many high on crack and cocaine, the place was like a Hieronymus Bosch scene on a psychedelic canvas, surreal, yet tangible and deadly.

The drugs wore off about four a.m. The calm was broken by the night guard giving me a 4:30 kick in the ribs, using the same tired line, "You got court this morning, Woltz. Don't want to keep the judge waiting."

I waited for hours to be transported a few blocks to the Eastern District Federal Courthouse and many hours more once there.

As we entered Judge W. Earl Britt's courtroom in our striped prison suits, we saw Mother, Jim, Robert Cook, and other loved ones scattered throughout in support. Tolly was seated at the defense table, along with my wife's attorney, former prosecutor, Donald Tisdale.

Judge Britt wound up quickly and told AUSA Matthew Martens to explain why we were brought to his court again, though it was Britt himself who ordered us there according to the docket sheet. Martens said he was "concerned about Mr. Woltz getting quality representation," and government decided to look into Mr. Kennon's activities to see if he was up to the task. Lo and behold, they determined he was not.

For the first time, I sat before a judge accompanied by an attorney of my own choosing. By day nine, Tolly had filed motions on my behalf and demanded to see the evidence against us, the same things I had begged David Freedman to do for half a year, and he did these things the first day without being asked. Their scheme would unravel before a truly adversarial process and a real defense attorney. Judge Britt or AUSA Martens (more likely both) decided to stop us before it was too late.

The Sixth Amendment not only guarantees the right to counsel, it includes the right to *choose* one's counsel, so long as he or she can afford it. This came about in a string of Supreme Court decisions beginning with *Powell v. Alabama*, 287 U.S. 45 (1932), through *Gideon v. Wainwright*, 372 U.S. 335 (1963), ending with *United States v. Gonzalez-Lopez*, 548 U.S. 140 (2006). The final case, *Gonzalez-Lopez*, was argued before the Supreme Court on the day of our arrest and remained in the news. The case was decided June 26, the day law required us to be tried, and was in effect by October 2, of 2006 when Judge Britt decided to violate it. He ignored the Supreme Court's ruling, and decided I needed a lawyer of *his* choosing rather than mine.

He looked around the courtroom as if searching for a lost kid at a county fair. "Is there anyone here who would consider representing Mr. Woltz?"

He craned his neck looking to the back, while asking me again if I was sure I had the needed representation. I assured him, on the record, Tolly A. Kennon III was the only attorney I wanted or needed.

A young attorney stood up in the back of the courtroom and asked to approach the bench. In a high-pitched voice, former AUSA Matthew J. Hoefling, announced to the court he was ready to come on board.

I asked Tolly, "Who the hell is that?" but he didn't know either.

Judge Britt assigned the prosecutor as part of my "defense" team over my objections that day, in violation of federal law.

My wife nervously rose to her feet and told Judge Britt she must have new counsel as her attorney, Mr. Tisdale, refused to prepare for trial.

The Judge viciously jumped at my wife with a snarl. He said unless a lawyer who was willing to represent her was in the room *at that moment*, no changes of attorney would be allowed "for the duration of the case." Judge Britt's illegal actions were matched only by his shocking display of abusiveness. Acting without any constitutional authority in our case, he ordered us to his foreign jurisdiction and venue to violate federal law himself by ruling on AUSA Martens' self-serving motion. His message was clear to all present. No attorney could challenge his lawlessness and participate in his courtroom. He berated my wife while making his point. He then assured all, that no zealous representation or adversarial process could take take place in his court by his actions. Our representation would be restricted to a former prosecutor, and team player of his choosing, one unwilling to challenge the bench.

Vernice was devastated. At the end of that long day, we were taken back to the Wake County Jail, where there was plenty of writing on the wall.

Visible through the barred window of the Yellow Pod on the scrolling electronic marquee of WRAL TV were the headlines of the day's news, including Sam Curin:

"FORMER U.S. ATTORNEY PLEADS GUILTY TO TAX FRAUD"

Sam took a deal from Martens and Judge Britt that day. His conviction could still be derailed if my challenge of Judge Britt's jurisdiction and venue violations was heard, and they knew it. Britt and Martens were taking no chances. Tolly Kennon would not play ball with them, so he would have to be destroyed and replaced by a prosecutor who would do their bidding. My "honest man" would be ruined for doing his job and following the Professional Code of Conduct. Perhaps that is why old Diogenes had so much trouble finding an honest man. They don't last very long, especially in a United States District Court of today. Those with absolute and unchecked power don't tolerate them.

There was little question Sam would do whatever he had to do to keep from going to prison, and Judge Britt could take advantage of this. As U.S. Attorney in Britt's court, Sam, by his own admission, sent many innocent men to every federal prison in the region. As a State Judge, he was known as "Maximum Sam" because he gave the highest sentence allowed in most cases. Sam would not likely survive a state or federal prison in the area.

I watched the WRAL-Sam Currin newsreel scroll by for a whole hour and pondered how it was possible for things to get worse.

CHAPTER 23

THE BROKEN RECORD

"A court cannot confer jurisdiction where none existed and cannot make a void proceeding valid. It is clear and well established law that a void order can be challenged in any court."

Old Wayne Mutual L. Association v. McDonough, 204 U.S. 8, 27 S.Ct. 236 (1907)

October 19, 2006 – Western District of North Carolina

My first meeting with the prosecutor cum defense lawyer, assigned by Judge Britt, was held on this day. Matthew J. Hoefling was on his way home for the weekend and had a young lad in tow, one with less than his own tender years. Hoefling said he was "just in training." To my chagrin, I later learned from an internal e-mail that this youthful trainee was not yet licensed when he came to defend me. He wrote, "I am being sworn in tomorrow, but do not have a bar card."

This was the "experienced criminal defense litigation team," for which Jim paid hundreds of thousands of dollars, on the order of Judge W. Earl Britt, comprised of a prosecutor who had never defended a soul in his life and a boy without a bar card.

The response from Associate, Antoine Robinson, to the trainee stated: "After speaking with Officer Paul Williams, he indicated that in order for you all to gain access you will need to bring him a large pepperoni pizza….I'm not kidding, this is what he said. AR"

The firm's "experienced criminal defense litigation team," was made to pay a petty bribe to get into the jail.

Tolly and I arranged a meeting at 2 p.m. that afternoon to plan trial strategy. Hoefling and his young trainee crashed the party. I asked Tolly to prepare a complaint against Martens for prosecutorial misconduct, including his April 27 admission he *shopped* Judge Britt and orchestrated the appointment due to his bias. This was the prelude to filing a judicial complaint against Britt as well. Thinking attorney/client privilege protected our conversation, I did this over the monitored jailhouse phone system, which proved to be a bad idea in Charlotte where federal laws and the Constitution are treated more like discretionary *guidelines*.

We later learned Martens received recordings of all my calls from jail. Martens pre-emptively attacked Tolly to prevent his filings of prosecutorial misconduct charges. Martens then sent my new court-forced attorney, who had worked with him as a prosecutor until a few months before, to press his case. Tolly was effectively sidelined, but I refused to let him go as my attorney.

From the day former AUSA Hoefling arrived, I knew he was working for others, not me. He opened the conversation by saying, "Now Mr. Woltz, I know from what your brother told me that you don't want to even hear the word 'plea', and I can appreciate that. I also understand that you're not enthusiastic about us having discussions with Matt Martens at the U.S. Attorney's office. But I felt it was my duty, as your attorney, to explore all avenues thoroughly, so I took the liberty of going to meet with Mr. Martens before coming over here, and I've got to tell you, I think that with all the evidence against you, you should consider taking his plea offer."

His message was the same pathetic one Freedman had served up. What he "understood" wasn't exactly clear to me. The best I could respond in the blush of new acquaintance was, "You what?"

Tolly and I locked eyes, each knowing the other's thoughts.

We later confirmed that the first thing through our minds was how this guy could possibly have reviewed any "evidence" when *we* had been prevented from seeing it for the better part of a year. That troubling question had but one answer. Only a *prosecutor, who was actively working on the case,* had access to those files.

As there was no immediate response, I continued. "You were instructed not to have any plea discussions, any at all with prosecutor Martens, yet you did so before we ever met? We're going to trial, Mr. Hoefling."

"It's my duty as your attorney, Mr. Woltz, to explore every avenue…"

"I know, I know," I said, cutting him off. "I heard all that. That's why I got rid of the last attorney, Mr. Hoefling. But is it not also your *duty* to follow client instructions?"

"In order to advise you properly, Mr. Woltz, we need to know all of the alternatives, and I really think with all the evidence against you, you should consider…"

I interrupted him again, "How do you know about 'evidence' against me, Mr. Hoefling, when *I* haven't even been allowed to see it? My last attorney let Martens sequester it. How could you have seen anything to make such a determination?"

Hoefling glanced at Tolly. The cover was off. This assistant U.S. Attorney had worked on my case *for* government.

He stammered, red-faced, "Well, I, uh, I think Mr. Martens said something about there being quite a lot of evidence."

"So we should just take the prosecutor's word for it and go ahead and sign a plea? Is that your recommendation, Mr. Hoefling," I asked sarcastically.

"What if I told you I never committed any crime, and they admitted that to me? Would pleading guilty still be your recommendation?"

"Mr. Martens certainly thinks you did," he replied with a poorly placed chuckle. I didn't see any humor in this attorney refusing to consider innocence before we spoke the first time.

"Just out of casual interest, what great deal did you negotiate with the prosecutor, Mr. Hoefling?"

"He's offered you a deal of fifteen years, and I think you really ought to…"

Tolly and I burst out laughing.

"Fifteen years!" I yelled. "You think that's a good deal? I turned down seven maximum as outrageous just last month, and you think I'll take fifteen for a crime I never committed? That, Mr. Hoefling, is why you were instructed not to talk to Mr. Martens. You just cut any bargaining position we may have had right out from under us by going to him to discuss a 'plea' before you ever met me. You were told for a reason not to do what you've already done."

"He's awfully angry at you over that letter you wrote Judge Britt," Hoefling retorted, in defense of his fellow prosecutor.

"That's why it's not the time to talk to him, Mr. Hoefling. That letter to the court was reporting his illegal conduct as a prosecutor. Do you expect that to make him happy?"

The alternate rosy and red facial complexions were part embarrassment, part anger. It was clear Martens did not tell him I refused half his "deal" just one-month prior, making Hoefling look like a fool.

And so it went at every meeting with Hoefling. I ordered him to help Tolly prepare for trial, review the evidence, file a motion for dismissal of the indictment under the Speedy Trial Act, and challenge my illegal incarceration. He ignored me just like David Freedman, pushed aside Tolly's involvement, and pressed for a plea of guilt.

A prosecutor is precluded from representing a defendant in the same matter just as a firm is precluded from pursuing representation if that prosecutor is later hired. Violating this rule warrants disciplinary action under the Professional Code of Conduct, Rule DR-9-101, previously noted. Hoefling joined Helms Mulliss Wicker (now McGuire Woods) shortly after being appointed to the case by Judge Britt, which precluded any of them from being my attorney under this rule.

Not only did Matthew J. Hoefling stand in violation of that mandatory disciplinary rule, so did the young lawyer who was with him, as well as the firm for which they worked. I wanted only Tolly to represent me.

The deputy came to run them out at 4:30 p.m. As soon as the guard deposited me upstairs, I tried to call Tolly. There was no answer.

The assignment of Hoefling to my case was both desperately not wanted, but also illegal, something we did not know at the time. It was understood we had to comply with Judge Britt's assignment and order that counsel could not be changed.

The next week crawled by.

When Friday afternoon rolled around, the guard called my name and took me downstairs. There was a not-so-instant replay of the week before.

Almost the same words and meeting format were used. Tolly was in a trial all week and unreachable. I asked him to come early the following week so we could meet alone. When he arrived, I asked why he was letting them run the show. He said, "Your brother asked me to let the 'big firm' take the lead."

About that time, in walked Hoefling, early as well, and asked, "Are we interrupting something?"

"Actually, Matt, I was telling Tolly I'm not satisfied at all with how this is going. You were hired, on order of Judge Britt, by my brother, not me. But as your client, I have ordered you to prepare for trial. You refuse to consider it, from everything I can see so far…"

He interrupted, "I think the plea agreement is very reasonable and that you really ought to…"

I had enough of his drivel. "Then you take it, damn it! You do fifteen years! Let me tell you something, Matt. I didn't break any law. I didn't…"

"Well Mr. Martens certainly thinks…"

"Stop right there! If you want to talk about a plea or what your friend Martens thinks, then you do it on your own damn time. You'll not waste one more minute of my time or money talking about it. We're going to trial. If you can't do that, then I need someone who can and will. Do you understand me?"

"I think you should really consider…"

"Are you deaf, Matt? I've listened to your nonsense for weeks now. You're like a broken record. Maybe this *defense* business isn't your thing. But if you're going to continue as my attorney, you're going to have to learn it," I said like the father I was old enough to be.

I turned to Tolly and said, "I can't take any more of this, Al. If these boys can't or won't do the job, you stay in the lead on this thing and start filing those motions."

He nodded in agreement.

"And Matt," I said, "I'm going to have Jim send copies of my instructions again. You seem to be ignoring them. I want to make sure that you can never say you did not have them. I want to challenge the grand jury, challenge this crazy Eastern District venue and Matt Martens' judge-shopping…"

"You shouldn't call it that!" Hoefling said in his pal's defense.

"I wouldn't if I hadn't heard him admit it himself!" I shouted back. "Whose side are you on, Matt? I'm having a very hard time telling."

He didn't respond, so I continued.

"I heard the man brag to David Freedman and a roomful of government agents and lawyers he couldn't believe he was able to get Sam Currin's 'blood-feud enemy of thirty years,' to agree to hear the case. It came out of his mouth, Matt. That's judge shopping, and it's illegal. I intend to challenge it."

"All the judges in the Western District recused themselves because of Sam Currin," he began. "That's why they had to look elsewhere for a judge, because the ones here all had a conflict."

"Did you really just say that? Listen to yourself. The *Western* District judges had a conflict because they 'knew' Sam when he was U.S. Attorney in the *Eastern* District and that's a conflict, yet Britt *presided* over Sam's own court in Raleigh and that's not? You've got to be kidding me, Matt. You're actually buying that crap?"

The boy's relationship, in all his stupidity, gullibility, and unquestioning nature, to his former bosses, was that of master and servant. It was too much to take.

"Sam was the U.S. Attorney in Judge Britt's own court," I continued. "Did Martens not tell you? You're trying to tell me every judge in the entire *Western* District recused himself because Sam Currin was an *Eastern* District U.S. Attorney in Judge Britt's court, yet Britt has no conflict and they do? No appearance of impropriety there, Matt? Maybe Mr. Martens failed to fill you in on that bit of history. Did he tell you that Sam Currin was Senator Jesse Helms' top aide in 1980, and it was his job to prevent one W. Earl Britt's confirmation by the U.S. Senate? You don't think Britt remembers, and that is why Martens chose him?"

By his clear reaction, I recognized Hoefling knew none of this. Martens never told him of the feud between Currin and Britt or of the animosity that grew larger between them when Sam was U.S. Attorney there.

"There isn't any way Mr. Martens could have chosen the judge, I can tell you that," Hoefling said but without conviction.

"Let's find out," I said. "Let's challenge it. I guarantee you I'm right. I'll bet anything this was not a regular appointment. I heard Martens say it himself!"

"I don't think you're right."

His defense was weakening. For the first time he was actually seeing the truth. AUSA Martens had been keeping secrets from his pal.

"Then prove me wrong," I said. "I wrote Freedman a letter about it when it happened. You have those letters, read them."

Freedman had my writing about the events, as did Hoefling. I wanted it all challenged, demanding each conflict exposed and every misconduct prosecuted. Hoefling knew all this. Jim forwarded the Freedman letters of instruction the day after Judge Britt assigned him the case. Those letters held his instructions of hire.

Only Tolly Kennon was ever willing to file charges of prosecutorial misconduct, and he was being preemptively destroyed by AUSA Martens, the target of that complaint, for preparing to do so.

My letter of instruction to these attorneys was explicit. I wrote:

"I'd like to immediately file charges of judge shopping and use that as part of our motion for change of venue to the Middle District. All of you have said

that Judge Britt and [Sam] Currin are old political enemies from back when he
was head of the Republican Party.

If all of you knew that, why on earth would all of you agree to drag a
Western District Case, through the Middle District (where it should be), down
to the Eastern District, to put us before a judge that really does have a conflict?"

Hoefling was reluctantly coming around to the truth, though it
pained him to do so. "Our associate at the firm, Bill Mayberry, used to
clerk for one of the judges. He knows the Clerk of Court. Maybe he
can find out," Hoefling said.

"Then let's do it. Let's turn this thing around!" I said
enthusiastically and with a slight glimmer of hope. My protestations
remained constant. "I didn't do anything. I didn't break any law, and
the evidence will prove it, if you will ever get it released so I can show
you. I'm not going to prison for something I didn't do without a fight!"

It took six or seven weeks, but that day for the first time we finally
communicated a few sentences and understood each other. My
expectations could not have been clearer. To be sure Hoefling knew
what to do, Jim sent a second set of the same instruction letters. I got
confirmation from his ever-efficient assistant, Kelly Kiser. The boys
had received their marching orders, twice.

No one with any intelligence or integrity could misunderstand what
was said or written. Or so I reasonably thought.

CHAPTER 24

WRONG AGAIN

"*A lawyer shall not intentionally fail to seek the lawful objectives of the client...*"

Disciplinary Rule 7-101, Representing a Client Zealously, Rules of Professional Conduct.

November 29, 2006 – Western District of North Carolina

My euphoria did not last long. It was as if Hoefling never heard a word. Next Friday's drive-by session was my *Groundhog Day*. He obtusely refused to consider instructions or orders of hire and went back into his fevered pitch each and every Friday. He and his young associate came on October 26, November 3, November 17, and November 29. By November's end, my patience had ended as well.

Each meeting he tried to convince me fifteen years in prison was a 'great deal'. At my age, fifteen years felt like a life-sentence. On this visit he added it would soon be removed from the table if I did not take it.

"Good." I replied, "Tell Martens to do it soon, so I don't ever have to hear you bring it up again, Matt. If you want to run on about Martens' fifteen year plea, turn off the clock, and we'll do it on your time."

There was a momentary pause, but he started again. I tapped my non-existent wristwatch.

"Don't do it."

The meeting ended. Hoefling's intransigence hit the two-month mark. Our accomplishments were few. We were no closer to preparing for trial. My patience exhausted.

I called Jim that evening and told him Hoefling refused to prepare for trial or follow my instructions. He was tired after a long week, but listened patiently.

"Why didn't you tell me this before?" Jim asked.

"I didn't want to seem like I couldn't get along with *all* lawyers. I don't have any problem with Tolly Kennon," I told him. "If these young boys would listen to him, I'd be better off, Jim. He knows what he's doing. He's also a fighter, but these guys have pushed him aside. Tolly said you wanted them to take the lead."

Jim confirmed the instructions to Tolly. "Plus," he reminded me, "Judge Britt ordered you not to change lawyers, so we're stuck with these guys."

Jim moved on to better news. He had received a communication from one of my clients in France who knew of our predicament and recommended a good attorney in Tampa. "Judge Britt didn't say the family couldn't hire a *consultant* attorney though, did he?"

"No he did not," I replied and smiled. Jim could always be counted on to think outside the box. He tracked down Jack Fernandez and paid yet another retainer to ensure the assigned did their job.

Before this conversation ended, Jim brought up the obscene bill he received from Hoefling. It seems his silent "trainee" trained at the rate $185 per hour. Why it was necessary to have him on the "experienced team" and for us to be expected to cover his time and expense, not the firm, was unjustifiable and outrageous.

This law firm proved to be disreputable in its dealings, from beginning to end. They billed in excess of $30,000 for a handful of drive-by meetings during the eight weeks leading up to our complaint and would ramp up to over $250,000 before they were done. I got the pleasure of their ineptness, and they got the good fortune of our acquaintance.

Jim called the business partner of the firm and told him of my deep dissatisfaction with the young prosecutor and his expensive assistant. Rather than replace Hoefling with an experienced criminal defense litigator, as requested, the firm simply assigned a third attorney to the case, one who would prove equally useless. The cure for our complaint turned out to be worse than the disease.

On December 7, 2006 he arrived. This pudgy, jolly-type fellow bounced into the Friday meeting to announce he was now on the case and immediately turned to leave.

"Whoa. Whoa," I said. "Not so fast. How much trial experience? Who were the clients? What sort of cases? How many of them did you win? We were to finally have an experienced criminal defense litigator. If you're it, I want to know something about you." He babbled and burbled awhile longer, told me that he knew of my brother, Jim, in Roanoke, VA, through his wife's family. That was his response, without answering questions, so I repeated them.

My "experienced defense litigator" was one William C. Mayberry. He led next Friday's drive-by billing-op, which continued to include the trainee with no experience and the prosecutor, whom I asked to be pulled off the case. It was a disaster. This threesome, preferring to argue client instructions, managed to bill $730 per hour.

To add usurious insult to injury, they averaged roughly nine hours back at the office, chatting and meeting for every hour spent with me. Never did they follow a single client directive until Jim hired a consultant to oversee them.

Eventually Mayberry dropped the pretenses. He admitted his career as a criminal lawyer consisted of a single case involving drugs and a member of the Outlaws motorcycle gang.

"How does that prepare you for a case like mine?"

"It was a criminal case."

"I gathered that, Mr. Mayberry, but how did a motorcycle gang drug case prepare you for a financial trial?"

His explanations rode through obscure mumblings and ended up in Roanoke, VA. He threw out the name of his wife's family. I instantly recognized it.

My brother, his current paymaster, lived in Roanoke and had been married to a member of that family. Jim and Mayberry were ex-brothers-in-law, but Jim's marriage to Mayberry's sister-in-law, ended in divorce, which is not generally considered the best basis for good relations.

I was surprised Jim hired this man to be part of my defense, if he knew the background. Considering the other deceptions by the firm, it occurred to me perhaps they were less than honest about that as well.

"Does Jim know he hired his ex-brother-in-law, Mr. Mayberry?" I asked. "Did that not come up in your conflict check? I'm sure a firm of your size must do them."

His blush accentuated his skin problems, and he said something to the effect that he didn't really see how it mattered. It certainly mattered to me and would to Jim. The gargantuan bills Mayberry piled up were evidence of his complete disregard for fairness and probity. He had inside knowledge of Jim's success and the fact he could afford the fees, but Jim was not on trial, nor was he the ultimate paymaster. I was.

Each time they came, I warned Mayberry only one of them was to be paid. No more gang-billing, and I didn't want Hoefling, the prosecutor, there at all. Yet with each visit, Mayberry showed up with his twosome for another gang-billing and claimed to have forgotten. Although he was told the bill would not be paid, he continued this unethical practice until termination and billed us without regard.

I later learned the firm demanded two of my brothers sign guarantees of payment. The firm was milking the cow for all it was worth.

My experience with David Freedman exposed me to the ugly side of unethical behavior by an *individual* attorney. McGuire Woods displayed an even uglier side, of unethical *firm* behavior. What they did to us over the ensuing months was nothing short of financial fraud, and for six months after their termination, the firm invoiced tens of thousand more dollars, though fully paid up to the last hour.

When I told Jim our new, so-called, trial attorney was his ex-brother-in-law; he was livid, as expected. Mayberry failed to report the conflict to the firm or they failed to report to Jim that his ex-brother-in-law worked for the firm and was assigned to the case.

Jack Fernandez of Zuckerman & Spaeder was our sixth lawyer. He came to Charlotte immediately upon hire to review the dyspeptic relationship. We were still unaware Judge Britt's order against changing counsel was unconstitutional, or these boys would have been sacked on the spot in October rather than wasting our money trying to force them to do their job. None of the lawyers ever advised us Britt's order was illegal, while picking our pockets with his protection.

The first meeting was a free-for-all. I reiterated my instructions to Mayberry, including the immediate filing of a Motion to Dismiss the Indictment under the Speedy Trial Act, which §3162(a)(2) of that act, required the court to grant. By law, the bill-fest would have ended that day, had Mayberry followed this one instruction.

The meeting closed with a warning. "Don't ever show up here with more than one of you again, and only come when I call you. I don't need three of you to come and do nothing I ask you to do, when just one of you can come and ignore my instructions for far less money."

After Bill's billing-crew left, I turned to Jack. "What do you think? Is it as bad as I told Jim, or not?"

Jack had a shell-shocked look, raddled his head saying, "This is the most dysfunctional attorney-client relationship I have ever seen."

He then met alone with Tolly and me, and saw a functional client/attorney team, but Tolly's assistance dwindled. He would soon be forced to step aside due to AUSA Martens' undeserving attention.

Jack asked Mayberry, Hoefling, and the silent trainee to meet again. He began by doing something no attorney other than Tolly had done to date. He asked about the case and my life. The others had skipped opening details preferring the plea bargain endgame.

Jack had all of the appearances of being a real lawyer. He asked me to run through personal history. There was a family overview and the listing of accomplishments: Eagle Scout with God & Country

Award; Superior and Gifted Student Program at Western Carolina
University fifth and sixth grades; Boy's State; Natural Resources
Wildlife Commissioner for North Carolina; President of the
American-Caribbean Trade Association; Presidential Roundtable;
Senate Selection Committee, advisor to two prime ministers...and the
digression, a juvenile speeding ticket reduced to improper equipment.

Jack then reviewed the facts in the case and proceeded to build a
theory of defense, not a redoubling plan for acquiescence as the others
had perfected.

The billing crew was quiet. There was no screaming. There was
no shouting. There was no cursing. Their first silence provided time to
watch, listen and learn what a real lawyer could do as client advocate.
I was impressed with Jack's performance, as my aid and their teacher.
The contrast between the two could not have been starker: listening
versus browbeating, strategy verses compliance. Jack's homework
assignment was to collect the case evidence before next class visit. With
dismissal, the master left.

Throughout December, Jack nudged and cajoled and at times
embarrassed them into investigating the case. Their reluctant,
doubting approach was slow to change. It gave way as Jack forced them
through the evidence and into the late hours of the night. The session
exercises looked at the charges in relationship to my firm's actions.
They compared the 'evidence' redacted by government and the
record presented to the grand jury to actual tapes and originals. The
exculpatory statements on the tapes were missing from the transcripts
as "unintelligible," including lines where I told them we would not
participate in any "grey areas" or unlawful activities. There were two
separate records of the activities with the Nassau con men. I watched
Matt Hoefling's comprehension of our ordeal evolve with more than a
degree of self-satisfaction. His reluctant admission to the truth came in
December.

A Potemkin village is as convincing as it is real. Government
charges are as real as the force behind them. The temptation to
believe, to fold, even in the face of the forged, is real. Not only did the

documentary evidence, the transcripts, not match the tapes, they were altered to express criminal intent.

What Jack accomplished was due solely to his force of will and skill as an outsider. They had examined the record, fabrications, evidence, real and redacted, and perjured testimony. The curtain lifted. What they would see was the same story I saw daily regarding *many* other men in the machine. Perhaps one can see too much. They would not or could not defend me.

The limits of what the group could accomplish was reached. Jack was not licensed in North Carolina, and was therefore unable to officially act as my lawyer, but he knew someone who could and do so with great skill. He called old friend and North Carolina attorney, J. Kirk Osborn, one of the state's most famous criminal defense lawyers, someone who did not need to wave a publication upon arrival. Things were about to change.

CHAPTER 25

CAPITULATION

"I know you too well after all of these years together to expect you to say that you committed a crime you did not, or to lie about someone else to set us free. I accept that, but I will not survive this much longer. Once already I've been taken from this jail to die, and my heart will not take any more. These words are not intended to make you change your mind, only to let you know that I will not be there for our children when this nightmare finally ends. Here is what I want you to promise me you will [do] for the boys in my absence..."

Opening paragraph of letter received from my wife on January 16th

January 17, 2007

Internal memos from McGuire Woods law firm establish Jack Fernandez and I were still pressing Hoefling and Mayberry to prepare for trial as late as January 9 of 2007. Tolly Kennon had been sidelined by government's attack. Orchestrated charges were filed, rendering him ineffective. Before the court that week, Martens openly attacked Tolly, challenging his status as my attorney, but I offered resistance. The other attorneys from McGuire Woods were there to see the show. Mayberry asked me to testify *against* Tolly for government. It

was a strange request but one confirmed years later in a copy of Bill's
e-mail of January 7, 2007, at 11:55 a.m.:

"I am going to try to carve out some time today to talk to Howell
about the strategic ploy of sacrificing Tolly to buy more time. We'll see."

It was a short conversation. I told Mayberry I would not trade an
eyebrow of Tolly Kennon for every attorney employed by McGuire
Woods. Tolly was the most decent criminal defense attorney I met
during the matter. McGuire Woods, in my opinion, refused to actively
defend me because they wanted to keep the case going and continue
the billings as long as possible. Mayberry's memo to Hoefling and the
silent trainee about the Tolly "sacrifice" appeared to confirm that.
More to the point was the list of actions they were unwilling to pursue:
the Speedy Trial dismissal motion; Jack Fernandez e-mails of January 8
and 9 outlining the illegal acts and constitutional violations; government
misconduct including perjury by its key grand jury witness, J. Vernon
Abernethy; warrantless searches and seizures; and Sixth Amendment
violations. The "what" and the "how to" were fed to McGuire Woods'
"experienced criminal defense litigation" team by Jack. They were
provided information by which to see the facts, win the case, and secure
our freedom. The client instructions necessitated this direction. Despite
all apparent progress from the month before, the team imploded.

Matt Hoefling's January 9, 2007 response to Jack's memos came as
an internal note to Mayberry saying, "'comprehensive factual memo'
= here is the stuff they should have done and didn't. Why is he drafting
such a document anyway?" The answer was simple. Do your job.

But an event changed all of that, literally overnight, causing me
to capitulate. A female guard who knew us both entered my cell late
one night after lock down and said, "Mr. Woltz, this is not any of
my business, but you need to do whatever you have to do to get your
wife out of here. She's not going to make it. We already took her to
the hospital once. Her heart won't take being away from her children
much longer. You better do whatever you have to, and do it soon."

The next day I received the letter at the beginning of this chapter corroborating the guard's warning. It was a farewell with instructions on what to do for our sons after her death.

I made the call to the McGuire Woods lawyers on the morning of January 17 and told Mayberry to draft a plea agreement, with instruction it must be predicated on the immediate release of my wife.

Mayberry replied, "I don't think Martens will ever go for that."

"He'll do it," I said.

Bill wanted to argue about it, but I was in no mood. I yelled my instructions again so loudly the guard ordered me off the phone and locked me down.

Getting my wife out before my so-called principles killed her became my sole focus. At that point, I would have confessed to murder if that is what it took to set her free, which I suppose was the purpose of taking her hostage in the first place.

In short order, I was called downstairs. It was Team Bill with an agreement. AUSA Martens agreed to let her go if I would take the after-the-deal money laundering charge he tried to add in May of the previous year. His original slate of charges fell apart under minimal scrutiny except "conspiracy to defraud the United States government," the charge derived from the con men's visit to Nassau. For that, we needed only to play the tapes of the meeting and show the falsified transcripts made from them. That charge would be dismissed, some agent or prosecutor would likely lose his job, and Martens would be embarrassed.

With that bit of leverage, I ordered Mayberry and crew to put wording in the agreement making it clear the only reason for the plea was to free my wife, indicating the plea was made under duress. There was also the letter to David Freedman detailing Martens' breach of contract and prosecutorial threats due to my unwillingness to engage in plea-bargaining during our final meeting in July of 2006. This too substantiated my case for duress. At that moment, however, all I wanted to do was free Vernice before it was too late. These men were not to be trusted, so I had to see her freed *before* signing the agreement in the court.

Hours of arguing caused me to negotiate differently, for their obstinacy was never confused with assistance and help. I stated firmly: "Add 'as a condition of the Plea Agreement, the Government has agreed to recommend the immediate release of V. Woltz. This recommendation is made at the request of defendant H. Woltz'. If you won't do that, then I will deal with Martens myself."

They exploded, saying Martens would never agree to such wording; it sounds like an exchange of a hostage for my plea.

"That's all this is. I'm signing Marten's plea in exchange for the release of his hostage. Martens would sell his mother for my name on that paper. He'll do it."

With surprisingly little change in wording, the line appeared on page five of the agreement within hours.

I also needed Martens to admit I didn't know of Sam Currin and his clients' true activities, though I was being required to say just that in exchange for my wife's freedom. After another lengthy battle with Team Bill, I got wording added which said, "Government has advised me and I stipulate that these funds were proceeds of Mr. J's and Mr. K's fraudulent penny stock promotion activities. While, in the absence of evidence protected under U.S.S.G. §1B1.8 the Government could not prove what portion of these transfers were conducted with my knowledge, consent, and participation, I hereby acknowledge that I knowingly laundered or caused to be laundered more than $7 million worth of these funds."

Seven million dollars was the entire value of everything we held in trust for Sam Currin and his clients when I ended the relationship. Those assets were forwarded to their attorney when they refused to give source of funds information and that event was years before any charge of wrongdoing by government. I could not have known such things, and I wanted Martens to acknowledge it.

This wording was included on the last page and item 51 of "Factual Basis for the Plea," which I doubt has ever been read by anyone except me, but it is in there. "Government has advised me and I stipulate…" In other words, "They told me what to say, and I said it to free my wife."

AUSA Martens' bold strategy paid off. All he had to do at that point was get a judge in the Western District Court to accept the plea, and I would go to prison for a crime the agent leading the case admitted I knew nothing about.

McGuire Woods billed me $92,000 that month, claiming to Jim it was because of their extensive work crafting this one-of-a-kind plea agreement. Some years later, I obtained a copy of Mayberry's e-mail to Martens that day, which described what actually happened. It confirmed what was suspected; government provided the agreement, not McGuire Woods. Mayberry timidly states on evidence page HW00708, "our version includes a few additional changes to the boilerplate language in the agreement. We ask that you consider those changes as well. Best regards, Bill."

CHAPTER 26

A CHAMPION APPEARS ON THE HORIZON

"What they've done to your wife and you, Mr. Woltz, is far worse than what they did to the boys in the Duke lacrosse case. Here, they've violated every federal protection guaranteed a citizen charged with a crime, and they've done it right out in the open."

J. Kirk Osborn, Criminal Defense Attorney

January 25, 2006 – Western District of North Carolina

I t was a cold Saturday morning in January when Jack Fernandez, our consulting attorney, called Kirk Osborn at his home in Chapel Hill, North Carolina to tell him about our case. Kirk immediately got in his car and drove three and a half hours to Charlotte.

This wonderful man did not know us. He came unbidden and unretained on January 18 to see my wife. She was literally dying of a broken heart.

Kirk gained the national spotlight in the case of the wrongfully charged Duke University lacrosse team by Durham, North Carolina prosecutor, Mike Nifong. This prosecutor knowingly hid exculpatory evidence, encouraged lying by witnesses, and set about destroying these young men for personal fame and glory.

Mr. Nifong's misbehavior sounded dreadfully familiar to us. Kirk and two other attorneys were relentless in their pursuit of the corrupt prosecutor. They exposed his illicit activities, causing an international outcry for his removal. Nifong hired a prosecutor's best friend, David B. Freedman, my old attorney, to protect his law license. Bad choice. He was summarily stripped of his position and license in a very public and humiliating way. At least David did not discriminate. It appears he represented Mr. Nifong as well as he represented me.

Kirk Osborn proposed doing to AUSA Martens et al, the same thing he did to Mike Nifong, once Vernice was free. He confidently stated he would get our plea agreements overturned based on the jurisdictional violations and prosecutorial misconduct employed to coerce us into signing them. A week after Kirk visited my wife, he came to see me with Jack Fernandez. His first statement was, "This is the worst case of government misconduct I've seen in my career."

I asked if that included his Duke lacrosse case and Mike Nifong, He replied, "What these people have done to your wife and you, Mr. Woltz, is far worse than what they did to the boys in the Duke lacrosse case. Here, they've violated every federal protection guaranteed a citizen charged with a crime, and they've done it right out in the open."

Coming from J. Kirk Osborn, this was strong medicine. From the moment he strode into the conference room that day, I knew he was someone of substance with whom our adversaries would have to reckon.

Kirk was a silver-haired, handsome gentleman, somewhere between Gregory Peck and Sam Waterston but with a more commanding presence. When he was in the room, all others became bit players and extras. I alerted Jim our champion was on the horizon. He immediately scheduled a meeting with Kirk and Jack in Charlotte.

The three of them met with AUSA Martens. Kirk told Martens he was to immediately schedule a plea colloquy where Vernice Woltz would be released, no ifs, ands, or buts. When finished, Jim told me Kirk simply rose and strode out as he had entered.

All of this was done within days. The only delay from that point forward involved my own lawyers telling me what Kirk proposed could not be done.

They returned, insisting they deal with Martens instead of Kirk, I firmly believe, so the bill-fest could continue. I told them, "Martens will do whatever Kirk says. Everything about this prosecution is illegal. The charges themselves were illegitimate, as even Hoefling here has finally admitted, and we're before a judge two jurisdictions away who has no authority in the case." Kirk explained at our meeting jurisdictional defects could not be waived, even by a plea agreement.

I caught a cautionary look between Mayberry and Hoefling. What had I said to prompt such a warning between them but the matter of the judicial appointment!

Hoefling had agreed to ask "his associate" about my accusation of judge-shopping AUSA Martens bragged of with the Western District Chief Clerk, "Johnsy." Bill Mayberry once clerked for a judge. There was enough inside knowledge between the two of them to sleuth the challenge.

"By the way, Matt, what did your 'associate' find out about the judge-shopping? I was right, wasn't I?"

Mayberry's face answered the question.

"How about it, Bill? What did your friend the Clerk say?"

He and Hoefling exchanged glances again, and finally he replied, "OK, Johnsy [Frank G. Johns, Clerk of Court] said that it wasn't a 'normal' appointment. Are you happy?"

" 'Not normal' means judge-shopping," I said.

"He would only tell me that it was *irregular*," Mayberry said.

"Judge-shopping, just like I said. Have you reported it yet?"

"I have no indication that it was illegal, just that it was *irregular*," he said.

" 'Irregular' as in the unlawful denial of due process and in violation of the Sixth Amendment?"

I took the minor win on the field, and let it go. Kirk would do this job. The case was his, not theirs, and I said so.

The day we executed the documents, January 26, 2007, was exceptionally cold. IRS Agent David "Scott" Schiller was waiting downstairs with a female agent and a large, young, gun-toting giant to escort us to the meeting. It was little consolation that Schiller had once noted the falsity of it all.

Once in chains I took satisfaction in knowing this was the last time I would see Vernice treated inhumanely. Martens' meeting was at Hoefling and Mayberry's offices on North Tryon Street, just up from the jail. The agents were bundled in thick coats, scarves, hats and gloves. Agent Schiller commanded a heavy Navy Pea Coat.

We, on the other hand, were in jail pajamas, clothing that couldn't keep us warm inside the jail. My anger rose at the agents' complete lack of humanity, as they chatted about whether the temperature would exceed 20°F that day.

As we rode down the street, a bank sign displayed 15°F. The agents were disorganized and struggled to find parking and put me out with the armed agent, keeping Vernice with them. I took no comfort or warmth from being handcuffed under the watch of a behemoth and his large gun as I stood in bright orange prison pajamas on the corner of Tryon and Eighth Streets, a frozen traffic cone in rush hour. Cars inched by. Their exhaust hung on us. It too felt frigid.

Drivers and passengers stared briefly from arm's length. Their eyes averted before we could affix. I would have done the same a year before. This was a surreal moment, equal parts fact and fiction. I was on my way to confess to a crime I did not commit so Vernice could be freed. There was a truth in there, somewhere; but I wasn't seeing it, not here, not now and not in my country.

Hypothermia began. The agents' car pulled up fifteen minutes later. Half a block down the street, we entered another parking garage. Once on its open deck, however, none of the three agents were sure where to go. This time, they put Vernice outside of the car with me while they conferenced. I demanded she be put back in the car until they figured out where they were. They did, but left me alone outside.

By the time we got in the building, I could not speak or move my hands. Jim, my brother, was there, as always, and with clothing, both making us briefly warmer and more human.

Schiller objected and announced our dress was a "security risk". We settled for wearing a sweater over our pajamas. By then it was mid-morning, but Martens was absent for his own meeting.

Vernice and I met with Jim and Kirk to review strategy. While waiting for Martens, Hoefling interrupted us several times, only to make excuses for him. It was apparent Martens and Hoefling were updating each other. Something else was up.

Martens dragged in that afternoon, seven hours late. An *Information* had been added to the plea agreement creating a new charge. The number 5:07-cr-3 was written in by hand, as if a strange incursion.

Every Charlotte Division case I had seen, which was quite a few by then, began with the number "3." Mayberry and Hoefling wouldn't tell me why the number was different on the *Information*. Something was wrong, and my initial reaction was to back out. But next to me appeared a frail dying body, and our intermittent contact told me so.

Kirk, who officially represented only Vernice, not me, advised me to sign knowing within weeks we would be able to void the agreements on the jurisdictional issue.

The plan was simple. First secure her safety and freedom then Kirk's efforts would begin in earnest. Since our conversation, he had confirmed the jurisdictional defects were not something that could be waived by plea agreement. A court either has jurisdiction or it does not, and the Eastern District Court of Judge Britt may as well have been in another country. Kirk said that day if we were taken to Raleigh in lieu of a colloquy in Charlotte, this helped our case as Judge Britt had no constitutional authority to accept the pleas either.

The bargain was made.

I was entering the loneliest days of my life. Having my wife in the same building two floors below kept my spirits focused. I could touch the wall in my tiny cell, and know that through the inanimate blocks, she was connected to me on the other end. That connection was ending. I was happy for her and our children but wondered, "Was Kirk too good to be true? Can someone really be taking up my cause after this nightmare?" I was signing a plea of guilt to uncommitted crimes for a sentence that could go as long as eighty-seven months, though I was told it would be far less, possibly "time served." I would be in my sixties before the terrifying dream ended, if Martens and Judge Britt had their way.

It was a hard pill to swallow, but I did so and signed the plea agreement.

CHAPTER 27

THE CONSPIRACY'S OBJECTIVE IS CONSUMATED

"In all criminal prosecutions, the accused shall enjoy the right to a speedy and public trial, by an impartial jury of the State and *district wherein the crime shall have been committed*, which district shall have been previously ascertained by law–" Amendment VI, United States Constitution

18 U.S.C. §3234 and Rule 20 of the Federal Rules of Criminal Procedure, Transfer for Plea or Sentencing. A prosecution can only be transferred to another court, if, 1) the defendant states in writing a wish to plead guilty and to waive trial in the district where the indictment, information, or complaint is pending, and files the statement in the transferee district and 2) the United States attorneys in both districts approve the transfer in writing.

February 6, 2007 – Eastern District of North Carolina

We were taken to Raleigh to go before Judge Britt for the required *plea colloquy*, though Rule 20, 18 U.S.C. §3234, and the Sixth Amendment precluded him from hearing it.

Statutory law and the Federal Rules of Criminal Procedure apparently made no difference to Martens or Britt. At these "colloquies", defendants are required to claim their plea is voluntarily given and tell the court they are pleased with the representation provided by their attorney. If a defendant is unwilling to parrot these statements, he or she will be sent back to jail, until willing to say so, true or otherwise.

On the way out of Charlotte, I wrested with a Boy Scout dilemma. If I didn't tell these untruths, my wife wouldn't go free. Would the return for lying alleviate all misgivings? When the judge would ask if my plea was voluntary, would it matter if he knew I was lying? If so, could I say it convincingly? The questions of principle dissolved superficially in the gauntlet that was Raleigh.

They put me in the Green pod on the fifth floor. This time, it was a near-death experience.

The usual middle of the night call came as the drug-infused crowd got drowsy, and a guard rousted me off the floor, telling me the judge was waiting. I was chained and placed in a holding cell for an indeterminate number of hours, as no clock was visible. We were taken in for the plea colloquy at the end of the day. Everything went smoothly until Judge Britt asked if anyone promised me anything in exchange for signing the plea. I hesitated, and turned to Bill Mayberry, "Of course they did. I was promised my wife would be freed or I wouldn't be here."

Before Mayberry could respond, Judge Britt realized his error and corrected himself, "or rather has anyone *threatened you*, Mr. Woltz, into taking this plea?"

I turned again to Mayberry, and said, "Of course they did. They threatened more charges against Vernice, if I didn't sign a plea." Martens had pointed to the new FBI agent that replaced Curran at our final meeting and threatened to pile more charges on her if I refused to take his new charge. Our agreement dated April 27, 2006, precluded additional charges against *me*, so he threatened more charges against *her* unless I *voluntarily* allowed it.

"But not *you*," Mayberry said, with a smirk. "He asked about *you*, not your wife." They had not threatened *me*, lately.

When I hesitated to answer Judge Britt's question, my wife squeezed my hand so hard it hurt. I choked back my anger knowing the day's purpose.

"No, your honor."

Judge Britt knew the statement to be false, as my letter to him on file in the case stated otherwise. The colloquy was simply for show, to give them both a record of my 'voluntary' plea and the coverage they needed.

The plea waived my right to appeal, so Kirk planned to attack the conviction on the basis that Judge Britt was biased and had no jurisdiction or authority to adjudicate the case in his Eastern District Court. That was enough according to Kirk.

I warned Mayberry before the colloquy began if they didn't release Vernice on the record, *before* I pled guilty; I would balk and refuse to finish it. I wasn't taking a chance on their promise. Mayberry passed the condition on to Martens as we waited for the proceeding to begin. The glare Martens sent back satisfied my concern for how well Mayberry conveyed the demand.

Judge Britt started with *my* plea colloquy, just as I feared, so Mayberry was again warned to do something or I would stand up and blow the whole charade. He jumped up and interrupted Judge Britt mid-sentence.

"Your Honor, may I be heard just briefly?"

Judge Britt replied, "Certainly."

Mayberry mumbled something about my sentence being at the bottom of some guidelines range, and then got to the meat of the interruption, "And Your Honor, at some point I would like to be heard or just join in with Mr. Osborn on the release of Mrs. Woltz. For now, just say that it's a *key element* of this plea agreement from Mr. Woltz' perspective."

That was an understatement. It was the *only* reason I was there, and Judge Britt knew it. Martens glared long enough to realize I was going to blow this thing up if Vernice was not let go, right then. I would figure out some way to wait for an April trial with Rick Graves.

They agreed to dispatch with her release. Britt stopped my colloquy and completed Vernice's.

Jim and Kirk stood at the ready to whisk her out the door to safety, while I confessed to something they needed to hear. I took solace knowing its falsehood had won her release and yet maintained the imprint of our innocence.

To no one's surprise, they tied our pleas together. Had I balked at that point, they would simply re-arrest her.

Later I saw her in the Wake County Jail from the vantage point of my holding cell. She was preparing to leave. I saw the outline of her thin, boney body. The clothes Jill provided could not conceal nine months of starvation and solitary confinement. My beautiful wife had been twisted into a coat hanger.

Brother Jim took no chances. He personally flew her to safety that night, while Kirk Osborn kept watch back in Raleigh.

My wife was safe and our children had their mother.

CHAPTER 28

MY LIFE GOES ON TRIAL IN A HIGHER COURT

"Crime is contagious. If the government becomes the lawbreaker, it breeds contempt for the law."

U.S. Supreme Court Justice Louis D. Brandeis

February 6, 2007 – Evening – Eastern District of North Carolina

After seeing my wife's final wave good-bye through my holding cell window, I dropped to the wooden bench. My legs no longer supported me.

The exposure and hypothermia in Charlotte the week before took their toll. Only adrenalin got me through the day knowing I must get Vernice released. By the day of the plea colloquy, there was nothing left mentally, physically, or emotionally to keep me from collapse.

When we returned to the Wake County Jail, I was in trouble. My forehead burned, yet I could not stay warm. Before going into the cellblock, I asked the guard for an emergency medical form, and told him something was seriously wrong.

I filled it out on the spot, gave it back, and asked, "Please get me to a doctor tonight." Outside, the temperature was plummeting. The jail was filling up with the homeless and helpless who were intentionally getting themselves arrested to get indoors for the night.

Even with the overcrowding, room #8 on the outside corner of the building was empty. One of my friends from an earlier visit to Wake County, Oscar Medellius, helped me to it. It seems Oscar was Minister of Finance of Peru under President Alberto Fujimori, but moved to Wilmington, NC after Fujimori's downfall and was arrested by the U.S. government. Oscar warned me room #8 was very cold, which is why it was still empty. It had no insulation.

All I wanted was a place to be left alone and sleep. My own thermostat was so out of whack I couldn't tell hot from cold. Oscar came to check on me frequently and brought an extra blanket upon seeing me shake. I promised to call my wife's sister, Jenny, and let her know Vernice was safe. Oscar and another man helped me to the phone a short time before delirium set in.

I didn't remember external events from the next day or so except a cup of water Oscar left. It had a thin crust of ice on top of it when I tried to drink. The outside temperature was 8° F.

My other memories were not of this world. I experienced a series of dreams where my life was on trial. There were arguments, carried out in a court-like atmosphere, but in an ethereal setting. They played back and forth, just as if two sides were debating. One side wanted to let go and move on to the next phase of existence. The other side wanted to finish out this life. Those dreams are still lucid memories years later.

The *pro* side argued for the reunification with my family and remaining friends. I would also live so as to fight legal corruption. 'Why me? Why this ordeal?' had been answered months before.

The *con* side arguments, however, were darkly alluring. By choosing not to live any longer, I could quietly slip away, and move toward the next stage of life or incarnation. The siren's song was sweet and fetching. The unearned shame I was suffering would be left along with the shell of my body. All I had to do was let go of my grip on the thin thread of life, and the nightmare would end. The debate continued for the better part of three days and nights before coming to a final verdict. The scale could easily have tipped either way.

The argument for life won out in the end. I awoke the fourth morning knowing I had a purpose to fulfill. Life would not be as pleasant or easy, but I was determined to take these forces on without fear or hesitation. After this deep transformational experience, I committed to a new life. I determined then to never mourn the old one.

That three-day visit to the other world left me a changed man. I *had* died, in a way. A reformer was born from the banker's ashes.

A week after my request for "emergency" medical attention, and after all danger had passed, a guard opened the cell door and asked if I was still interested in seeing a doctor. I pledged at that moment to work tirelessly to bring reform to this cruel and destructive machine that ruins lives, families, and spirits.

CHAPTER 29

RUNNING THE GUANTLET

"Where a court failed to observe safeguards, it amounts to denial of due process of law, court is deprived of juris."

Merritt v. Hunter, 10ᵗʰ Cir., 170 F.2d 739

February 18, 2007 – Western District of North Carolina

T he only charge from the original indictment to have survived dismissal was *conspiracy to defraud the U.S. government*, and a jury trial was scheduled in the Western District for the first week of April. It was only six weeks away. Kirk was confident my alleged *co-conspirator*, Attorney Rick Graves, would be found *not* guilty, unless I agreed to falsely testify against him on government's behalf in exchange for a time cut. There had been no conspiracy to break the law, but Martens counted on my false testimony to convict Graves, as proposed on July 27 of the preceding year. He swore the FBI would be on my doorstep with indictments for us both for the rest of our lives if I did not.

There was no one else to testify, as only Rick Graves and I were accused. The charge against Sam Currin was dismissed as unsustainable and part of his deal. If I did not lie for government, Martens simply could not win the case.

According to Kirk, if Rick Graves were acquitted, that acquitted me as well, because there is no such thing under law as a *sole* conspirator. Although I was forced to plead guilty to it, the charge could still be overturned for two reasons:

1.) The Eastern District Court had no jurisdiction or authority to accept the plea. In other words, Judge W. Earl Britt violated due process and his court was "deprived of juris," as stated in the case law cited in the chapter heading; and,

2.) Case law was clear on what happened if Rick Graves were acquitted, according to Kirk. The courts have consistently ruled, "Where all but one of the charged conspirators are acquitted, the verdict against the one will not stand." (11 Am Jur-Conspiracy 26, Herman v. United States, 289 F.2d 362, 367 (11th Cir. 1961)).

Rick Graves' acquittal, acquitted me, thus overturning the plea. Without Vernice as a hostage, I would have never pled guilty to anything else, and they knew it.

Kirk also wanted to wait until Rick Graves' acquittal before raising the jurisdiction issue to prevent Martens from trying to hustle me into a courtroom in Charlotte that *did* have jurisdiction to hold another plea colloquy. If he brought Britt there, it might be deemed legal. That would remove our jurisdictional argument and make overturning the plea very difficult. The agreement I was forced to sign waived all rights of appeal with few exceptions. Only my claims of prosecutorial misconduct, ineffective assistance of counsel, and jurisdictional violations could be raised.

All I had to do was keep my head down and wait, according to Kirk.

Rick Graves' attorney, Peter Crane Anderson, was also a fine criminal defense lawyer. With such a weak case, Martens would be torn to pieces, according to Kirk. Peter had clerked for Judge Mullen and he would be protected from foul play if Martens ambushed him as he had Tolly Kennon.

Pete Anderson approached me about testifying *for* Rick Graves, but there was no need in my opinion, and only potential liability. Martens must have thought I would do so, however, because I was moved to the sleep deprivation pod (6500) two weeks before his trial was to begin. Witnesses against the government and those on appeal were housed there, subjected to twenty-four hour lighting and permitted a maximum of four hours sleep per day.

Our thin blankets could be used only during this brief period between midnight and 4 a.m. At that time each morning, the guard yelled for us to take our sleeping mats off the floor and put up our blankets in preparation for the 4:30 a.m. line-up and "feeding".

During the remaining twenty hours, we were not allowed to use our blanket, despite the cold temperature. Prisoners were required to sit upright or stand for the entire time. No reclining was permitted anywhere for any reason.

We joked about articles in the news regarding the torture of foreign prisoners in Guantanamo Bay and our nation's secret prisons abroad, wondering if the guards were trained in Charlotte. The tactics were the same.

Vernice and Mother came to visit me. They could tell I was not lucid. My wife spent many hours in the doctor's office while she was in Mecklenburg and knew the staff well. She called Dr. Wait, the jail's physician.

Fortunately, he acted. I was pulled out of the sleep deprivation pod just before Rick Graves' trial began, on Dr. Wait's order. I slept for the better part of the next two days.

CHAPTER 30

THE BEST LAID PLANS OF MICE AND MEN...

"Famous attorney, Kirk Osborn...."

News report, March 25, 2007, 7:00 a.m.

March 25, 2007 – Western District of North Carolina

Rick Graves was scheduled to pick his jury on April 2, 2007. I was on pins and needles despite believing a jury would do the right thing. Nothing could prepare me for what I heard after the doors to our cells opened that morning. The TV blared, "Famous attorney, Kirk Osborn of Chapel Hill, is in critical condition." I don't know what else the reporter said. I went stone cold.

Our entire strategy and my freedom rested completely with this fine man. He was suddenly near death, days before the trial, which was to have been the event that would free me as well.

According to the news, Kirk simply collapsed and was in intensive care. I could not believe that, as he was in good health and in his prime.

At that time of day no one was on the phones, so I was able to reach Vernice immediately. She was hysterical and could barely speak through her tears and anguish. Kirk became like a father to her after coming to our rescue. He called every day to give her hope and let her know he would soon have me free as well.

The day of his collapse, Kirk drove from Chapel Hill to Mt. Airy and took Mother to lunch. He explained the plan for my release. Later that morning I called her. She told me Kirk not only assured her we had committed no crime, but those doing this to us were about to suffer consequences for their misdeeds once the trial of Rick Graves ended. Mother's lunch with Kirk was just hours before his collapse.

After returning to Chapel Hill, Kirk was found in his office collapsed on my files, and died a death, which to my knowledge, has yet to be fully explained. He was the picture of health during our association.

Words cannot express what this warm and honest man meant to us. He was compassionate, decent, and an amazingly skilled attorney with the rare courage to stand for what is right.

I went into a deep and dangerous depression. All hope was gone in an instant. The following days were dark, and I craved sleep to escape. I knew of no one else with the courage to face these people besides Tolly, and he had been destroyed by government for possessing that same virtue.

CHAPTER 31

TRIAL WEEK

"The interest of the United States in a criminal prosecution is not that it shall win the case, but that justice will be done."

Jencks v. United States, 353 U.S. 657 (1957)

April 6, 2007 – Western District of North Carolina

Without Kirk Osborn, I was not sure what to do. I again requested a copy of the Non-Affinity Agreement Martens and David Freedman signed with me on April 27, 2006. That document precluded the addition of the charge forced on me the day of the plea agreement.

As early as August 29, 2006 I filed documents ordering my files returned, but David refused to disgorge them though required by law and the Professional Code of Conduct to do so. A complaint was filed with the North Carolina State Bar, but David refused to turn over my records even on their order. The State Bar then refused to force the issue. This and other experiences taught me the State Bar's purpose is, at least in practice, to protect attorneys from the public, not the public from bad attorneys. Such an organization is inept if it is unwilling or unable to fulfill this most basic of missions.

Bill Mayberry and his crew also refused my request for a copy of the Agreement, claiming that I had made a "deal," so it was no longer relevant. I later learned that breach of contract by government is always a reason for overturn of a plea (*Santobello v. New York - 404 U.S. 257 (1971)*), which I suspect is the real reason it was not given. Others wanted more billing opportunities; I wanted results.

Kirk's assessment of matters was concise and matched the Public Defender's warning to David Freedman at the bond revocation in Raleigh the year before. Judge Britt had no jurisdiction to hold a hearing, including a plea colloquy, and therefore any judgment of his court was void. Government and Judge Britt could be forced to live by the law. Two lawyers, one in the private sector and one in public, agreed. The legal arguments were there, but could I now find the right assistance?

With Kirk's death, unless Rick Graves was acquitted, I wasn't confident my solid case would be enough. I had no one to pursue the jurisdictional argument. Deprived access to the law library, it was hard to research the issues on my own. Going to prison for uncommitted crimes would be my fate unless there was someone to defend me and challenge the criminal conduct of the government and Judge Britt's foreign court.

Kirk mentioned legal cases *"Musgrave"* and *"Austin-Begley,"* which supported his position regarding the illegality of being a sole conspirator as well. I noted those names in my journal, never expecting to have to pursue the issue myself. I would have to file a motion for relief in the event Rick Graves were acquitted. That would be difficult because law library requests continued to be denied. Days later, Sheriff Pendergraph shut down the law library for everyone. Legal aid refused assistance.

"Ask your family," was their final reply to my request(s) for legal aid assistance.

McGuire Woods was unwilling to help. They appeared to be more foe than friend, doing the work of Martens and Britt, only I was paying them. Even Jack Fernandez, the consultant, faded from view after the death of Kirk Osborn. I was alone.

The tension built daily the week before Graves' trial, and I could not focus on anything else. My captors moved me three times that week to different cellblocks in an apparent attempt to keep me off base. Initially, it was stressful to deal with new and sometimes hostile groups, but by that time, I couldn't go anywhere in the jail without knowing someone or running into men I'd helped with cases. Meditation, which had been my salvation throughout, became impossible that week and the meager food rations went uneaten.

Once Rick's trial actually began, things worsened, but the government rested its case after a week and the jury began deliberations. Vernice, now released, did her best to curb my hopes for a *not guilty* verdict every day of the trial, which I found strange. By the day the verdict was expected, I had been shuffled to cell block 4200, my location before the sleep-deprivation pod.

I promised to call Vernice the afternoon of the expected verdict, but that became impossible. A Haitian man passed out from hunger while taking a shower just outside the door of my cell. It sounded like a pistol shot when his head hit the tile floor.

The female guard yelled, "Lock down," meaning all were not to leave quarters, but she was not doing anything to help the poor man. I left my cell and crawled under the locked shower door to make sure he was all right. His skin was cold. Water was spraying into his open mouth, literally drowning him.

The blow to the head was severe, and he was not breathing. The guard was still screaming, "lock down," rather than worrying about a man who was going to die.

"Call medical, NOW!" I screamed in return. I turned off the water, turned him sideways so the mouth could drain. He did not cough or breath, so I performed CPR to keep the blood flowing and restore breathing.

He choked and gurgled. The guard was still screaming, "lock down."

"Quit yelling and get medical up here, NOW!"

The man finally coughed up water and breathed, but appeared to be in shock. I remembered running bird dogs in field trials on warm days, and they sometimes went into this state from over exertion. They appeared almost dead, but it was usually a sugar deficiency. We kept corn syrup or sweet liquid handy to revive them. I unlocked the shower door from the inside and ran to retrieve a cup and a sugar packet saved from breakfast. I put the sugar to lip and wet it with water, massaging his gums so it would absorb. This took a few minutes. By the time I looked around, there were five or six guards and a wheelchair. They watched, not moving, in the protection of their latex gloves.

"Help me get him into the wheelchair and cover him up. He's in shock."

One of the female guards said, "I ain't touching no naked inmate," and the group burst out in laughter. No one moved to help, so I lifted the man from under his arms, dragged him into the wheelchair, and partially covered him in jail uniform and towel. "Get a blanket over him immediately. He must be kept warm. Tell them downstairs that he may be in diabetic shock."

I put in more sugar and water.

"He's breathing again, but still in shock, and may have some water in his lungs. He had a bad blow to the head and may also have a concussion."

Before going into the cell to lock down, I looked at the clock. The appointed time to call Vernice about the verdict had past. The phones wouldn't be turned on again until late that evening.

At 4 p.m., the doors to our cell doors opened for the evening meal. I was still wet from helping the man in the shower. The female guard stared without word. Would I be punished for not locking down on her order? There was no offer of a dry uniform. I finally asked how the man was doing.

"He's OK," she said with another long and uncertain stare and turned away.

After dinner, she locked us down but later came by.

"That was a nice thing you did for that man today. How did you know what to do?"

I didn't feel like telling her about bird dogs, or being an Eagle Scout or anything else, so I said, "I've been around. It just came to me."

"Hmph!" she grunted and closed the door.

Just before 7 p.m. she let us out for shift change and the fifth alphabetical roll call of the day, as if one of us could have escaped.

We suffered through the same boring orientation speech I had heard 720 times by then. Over half the pod didn't speak English, which made it all the more ridiculous. I tuned her out and watched the second hand slowly round the face of the cheap wall clock, waiting to make my phone call.

We were locked down until after 8 p.m. at which time the guard let us out, and the men ran for the few working phones. I lost the race.

The interminable wait for a phone passed. I dialed Vernice, and she answered the last ring before voicemail.

She told a summary of the week's events, a repeat of details we discussed daily. With my allotted time about to expire, I interrupted, "Please just tell me…did the jury find him guilty or not?"

"Howell, it really isn't going to help you. With Kirk dead and no one else willing to go against these people, it…"

"Vernice, please. Just tell me."

"I don't want you to get your hopes up, and you know how crooked these people are—"

The operator came on to warn that the phone call was ending.

"Vernice, please!"

There was a long pause. The wait continued. "The jury acquitted him, Howell, but don't get your hopes up, please. They are so corrupt it may not make any difference. They don't go by the law. We've seen that, and…"

Silence.

A jury in the Western District Court of jurisdiction, which by law, was an unreviewable decision, acquitted Rick Graves, my only alleged co-conspirator. That meant, by any reasonable measure of fairness and legality, I would be freed too. The jury determined there was no conspiracy.

Judge Britt would have to let me go. For the first night in a week, I went to bed and slept peacefully for surely the bad dream was over. I would go home a free man.

CHAPTER 32

JUSTICE DENIED

"Because an indictment is jurisdictional, a defect in an indictment is not waived by a plea agreement." *United States v. Berrios-Centino*, **250 F.3d 294 (5ᵗʰ Cir., 2001)**

May 4, 2007 – Western District

But things did not work out that way. During Vernice's next visit she informed me she had testified against Rick Graves for Martens. Her rationale was based on a deceptive promise by AUSA Martens to reduce or forego my sentence for her false testimony. She knew I was strongly opposed to such dealings, and did not tell me of her plans. I had taken a calculated risk to free her and wanted to believe her motivation for aiding Martens was the same; that she was trying to help me. Vernice told the jury "we" conspired with Rick Graves, though she had not been charged with that crime and knew nothing of our dealings. When I finally saw her testimony years later (in 2013), I was aghast. Judge Britt ordered the jury out of the courtroom and Vernice testified against me more than Rick Graves, which could only have been done on Martens' prompting, in my opinion, to prevent me from seeking to void the plea agreement or be ready if I did.

Aiding the prosecutor was the worst thing for me. It was a clear attempt to get my wife's testimony against me on record, but clearly not relevant to the case with the jury out of the room and she could have avoided it by claiming spousal privilege. When Martens lost the trial despite her testimony, he reneged on his promise to give me relief and sought revenge instead.

I had cost them a win by not giving false testimony against Graves, and my punishment was months on *diesel therapy*, a life of living hell, where a prisoner is ridden from jail to jail for no purpose other than to destroy him.

The pre-sentence report, the basis of sentencing, was a mess. Probation, in violation of the plea agreement, ramped up the amount allegedly laundered from seven million dollars, as stated in the Factual Basis, to "in excess of 20 million." This greatly increased my sentence, while violating our contract. Judge Britt could choose any sentence that fit those numbers. The probation department, which works for the judge, also added "enhancements" for things to which I never admitted and had not been found by a jury, although a string of court decisions beginning with *United States v. Booker* precluded them from doing so. Mayberry and Hoefling refused to file any objections, so I fired them on May 4, caring not what Judge Britt had to say about it any longer, and asked Tolly Kennon to help me the day before the deadline. He was more or less out of practice, but was not yet without license. He came to see me to offer last minute assistance.

Judge Britt dismissed our objections without hearing or review, as is of record in the case. None of the other attorneys challenged him, though not yet released from the case. This acted as an acceptance on my part I was later informed, and removed the unadmitted enhancements and violations of the plea agreement as issues for appeal or at sentencing. Judge Britt ordered me transported to Raleigh for sentencing on October 2, 2007, based on the faulty Presentence Report, again, and without jurisdiction or authority in the case. It was a sad day for Rule 20, 18 U.S.C. §3234, the Sixth Amendment to the United States Constitution, and me.

While being moved around prior to sentencing, I met Chavis Moore, another of Tolly's clients. He was government's witness against

Tolly, and admitted to me he was offered a time-cut to testify in the case. Chavis further disclosed that what he agreed to say was untrue, but did so in exchange for a fifty percent reduction in his sentence. He was required to say Tolly told his girlfriend "to leave town," so she could not testify against Chavis, when in fact, she called Tolly to ask if she could visit her mother in Philadelphia. Tolly correctly responded if she were not under indictment or told by the authorities not to leave town, then she was free to do so. I talked Chavis out of committing this crime for government and alerted Tolly by letter what Martens was doing. Government upped the ante and offered Chavis more time off. He agreed to the deal so he could go home. Tolly was eventually forced to *voluntarily* surrender his law license to avoid prison for something he had not done. I still feel responsible for this as, on information and belief, Tolly was destroyed when he began unraveling Judge Britt and AUSA Martens' scheme in my case. Getting two jailed informants to lie against a lawyer in exchange for a time cut was a simple matter. I know from personal interaction with one of them, the truth was not told and a good man was destroyed by the threat of false testimony, scripted by government.

One or both AUSA Martens and Judge Britt kept me on the move as much as possible after this. I don't know whether it was due to my dealings with Tolly or the fact that I refused to help them convict Graves, but days later, the night my *diesel therapy* started in May of 2007, I was set up for an escape charge. This sounds beyond the pale for those who have not experienced our system of justice, and I include this episode only because it is documented in my case (Docket items #238, 242, and 243). These documents have since been sealed on order of Eastern District Judge W. Earl Britt, but copies were kept. Those sealed documents tell the story, one Martens and Britt do not want told.

In the middle of the night, an unknown man came to my cell and opened the door. "You're leaving, Woltz," he said. "Pack it up. They're setting you free."

I asked where the guard was, and the stranger said, "She's gone on break. Come with me."

No one was ever discharged after 12 p.m. or before 7 a.m. According to the clock, it was 2:45 in the morning. I knew every guard in the jail by then, and this man was not one of them.

I told the stranger I wanted to give away my commissary items and used that as a pretext to give two friends notes while sliding items under their doors. I scribbled Tolly's address and phone number on two pieces of paper and wrote, "Contact Attorney Kennon and tell him what you heard." Paranoia convinced me I was about to join the mysterious "Mecklenburg Dead." At that point in 2007, an average of one inmate per month was dying in the jail, often under unexplained circumstances.

Two men, Ronald Adams and Allan Coffey, sent affidavits to Tolly regarding what they saw and heard that night. Tolly wrote of the night's happenings in a motion to the court. He learned the whole story later upon finding me hidden in Judge Britt's Eastern District. Britt stated in his sequestration order that I requested he seal the information, though filed by my attorney on my instruction to be part of the record on appeal. In other words, Judge Britt put important evidence of serious violations of law, under seal, so no one could see what had been done to me, including the appellate court, and blamed that act on me, the man who filed it.

I was taken downstairs and told to dress in street clothes. The stranger left and was seen no more. The night clerk prepared a cashier's check for my commissary account. Once dressed I saw the double doors open to the street. The night clerk said, "You are free to leave."

I have no idea what might have happened had I walked out that spring night in May 2007. Dressed in street clothes with a money order in my pocket, it was a tempting offer, but my radar was on high alert. The night clerk offered more encouragement.

"Go on, Woltz. Door's open. Go ahead. You're free."

"I need to see the release paperwork and get a copy of the court order before I walk out that door."

"Go on. You're free. You don't need that," the transplanted New Yorker said.

"Not until I get some paperwork." I sat down.

"Suit yourself," he said, and announced to a female property clerk he was going on break, opening the door behind his desk. She promptly announced she was going to the ladies room "for a while" and disappeared as well.

I was left alone in the discharge and property office of the Mecklenburg County Sheriff's Department at 3:30 a.m. with the exit doors open to the night, and not a soul in sight. Despite the many violent episodes experienced, I was never terrified until then.

It was a set up, one in which I was either to be murdered or charged with escape. It was another trap by the same dishonest people who put me here. If they could get me to leave without a release order, chances are they would avoid penalty for all of their wrongdoing, including whatever happened that night.

In minutes, their sergeant entered and looked around the room, then at me, then at the double doors left wide open to the streets and said, "What are you doing here?"

Before I could answer, he turned and shouted to the empty room, "Where is everybody?"

"We're here Sarge," said the night clerk, stepping out from behind the door.

"Right here," said the property lady, having only hidden behind her large counter.

"What the hell is going on?" he barked.

No one answered. He was apparently left out of the loop on the set-up, and didn't like it, as he would be left to take the blame.

"I'll tell you," I said, and quietly explained the events of the last forty-five minutes including what I thought was going on.

He was livid. He went to the computer and pulled up my name and file, and cut loose with a string of expletives. He ordered me into a small closet/toilet behind the duty desk, and closed the door, with the lights off, (unintentionally, I think). His tirade went on for some time. I could well understand his anger. This set-up could only be done with

Sheriff Pendergraph's knowledge and participation, but no one told the night sergeant.

"Who brought this man down?"

None of them knew him, and the stranger had conveniently disappeared.

For the next seven hours, I sat in the dark until the day-sergeant opened the door to the small closet.

"What are you doing in here?"

I told him the story and suggested he call AUSA Matthew Martens at the U.S. Attorney's Office if he wanted to know what was going on.

He did, and I could hear him say, "But this man hasn't even been sentenced. We can't send him to prison!" There was silence for several seconds. Then, "Yes sir. Yes sir," followed by hushed conversation after he hung up.

The suspense didn't last long. I was taken out of the closet, shackled, hands, waist, feet, and shipped by prison bus to the ancient U.S.P. Atlanta where Al Capone served time in the 1930s. U.S.P. Atlanta sits on the graveyard of a civil war prison camp. It was built in 1908, but is still in service. They had no record of me upon arrival, of course, not being convicted or sentenced, so I remained in holding until early the following morning. Eventually, a guard placed me into a two-man cell with a prisoner who was a deaf mute and another who couldn't be quiet. The deaf man rolled up old newspapers, stuffing them in the space under the door where food trays were passed in and taken out.

I drew a question mark.

He held up fingers to the side of his head like ears. There was nowhere else to sleep but the floor of the small cell by that door. I had to see if he was serious. One look out the tiny window of the iron door told me he was. A rat, easily as long as my forearm and hand, cruised down the corridor. An hour later, I was pulled out of the cell and put back on the road. By 10 a.m., I was in sight of the Mecklenburg County Jail, the same one I left the afternoon before. Next stop, FCI-Butner, then to Wilson County's condemned jail, then Louisburg, and so on. This was *diesel therapy*.

From there, I was shipped to every dirty jail and prison they could find. Twice again I went to Raleigh for sentencing before Judge Britt actually did so, but was put back on the road instead. On one of those trips to Raleigh, Judge Britt, via AUSA Martens, sent Jim Woltz into the U.S. marshals holding cell while I was meeting with Tolly. He was the only lawyer still of record in my case, one I wasn't about to give up.

It was July of 2007, but I had yet to be sentenced. Jim said he was sent by Martens and Britt to warn me I would spend fifteen years in prison if I did not fire Tolly. A record of this action is on the transcript of the proceeding. To my knowledge, this is unprecedented and certainly not lawful.

In October of 2007, I was taken again to Raleigh for sentencing. Martens violated the plea agreement by recommending an increased sentence based on an amount of money higher than was in the plea agreement. Judge Britt was happy to accommodate him and sentenced me to eighty-seven months in federal prison. I was immediately shipped to and sequestered in a private prison in the Dismal Swamp of Tidewater Virginia without access to law or phone, thus preventing my filing notice of direct appeal within the brief period allowed.

Their ploy worked. I missed the deadline.

I spent the next three months in Tidewater Regional Jail without access to law, recreation, or other rights guaranteed a federal prisoner. The jail was full of poor black men, many of whom did not know why they were being held. Several were there for years while the private jail billed the State of Virginia and federal government an exorbitant daily fee, rather than release or bring them to trial, as law requires.

According to an article in the local *Hampton Roads News*, the Tidewater Regional Jail was owned by three local judges. The jail was full. It appeared the judges were looking after their investment at the expense of due process and civil rights. I filed speedy trial dismissal motions for as many of them as I could. Some of their occupants were released. I was bad for business so they put me on the road to Oklahoma in the middle of night, December 25, 2007.

On the second day in Oklahoma a man tried to kill me. He was overheard saying to his friends he was not going to USP-Beaumont with a child-molestation charge on his sentencing sheet, as he would be killed. He decided he would go there for murder as the more recent charge, which would show on his sentencing sheet instead, and likely run concurrently with the child-molestation, and keep him alive. Our first altercation came when he attempted to jump the line in front of me. Later, he followed me to the cell where the real fireworks occurred. I managed to get out while locking him in. We were both arrested, but the cameras backed my version of what happened.

The counselor who interviewed me regarding the incident, Ms. Israel, asked why I had been rated "dangerous" by the Office of the U.S. Attorney in Charlotte, while nothing in my record indicated violence. Martens recommended Medium FCI in West Virginia, which held violent men and those with over ten years to serve. Ms. Israel said that was wrong and changed my security rating on the spot. Her action may well have kept me alive.

In the middle of the night, February 7, 2008, almost two years after arrest, I was put on a plane headed back East. It landed within a two-hour drive of Raleigh, where a new journey began.

CHAPTER 33

FEDERAL CORRECTIONAL INSTITUTION – BECKLEY, WV

"We tell ourselves a lot of lies about prisons. The biggest lie is calling it 'the criminal justice system'; it is not a system, it has nothing to do with justice, and if there is anything criminal about it, it's the fact that jails tend to make their inmates lifelong antisocial animals."
Ben Bova, author, circa 1999

February 8, 2008 – FCI-Beckley, West Virginia

After numerous stops, the well-worn Prison Air Transport jet landed in Lewisburg, West Virginia. We were loaded onto an old bus by a large man wielding a pump shotgun and locked in a cage for the ride to Beaver, West Virginia.

Once there, we were unchained, stripped, inspected, and given prison uniforms. I was interviewed by Case Manager Beverly Smith and Counselor John Grimes. Grimes looked up from my record and said, "You and I are not going to get along."

Ms. Smith asked my religion. I said, "Native American."

"You don't look Native American," she said, and refused to put it down.

"Are all Muslims required to be from the Middle East, and all Christians required to be from a Jewish background?"

That began my first battle at FPC-Beckley.

After processing, we were put in holding cells for a few hours. Two or three prisoners were called out at a time and sent to their housing units. I came from Oklahoma City with a nice young man named Cedric Bennett. He had a "grill" in his teeth, dreadlocks to his shoulders, and soft-spoken demeanor. We were called out together and assigned to the Camp, which was a lower security facility, thanks to the counselor in Oklahoma City. Unchained and unescorted, the guard ordered us out the door to a waiting pickup truck.

I had been under maximum security for almost two years and had not seen the out-of-doors except during twenty-five transfers between jails and prisons, always in chains. I thought this was another set up and refused to walk out the door. Cedric took me gently by the arm and coaxed in a calm voice.

"I believe it's safe, Mr. Woltz. Here, I'll go first."

We got in the old pickup truck with "Stubbs," the town driver, and went down a two-lane road, without chains, to Federal Prison Camp-Beckley.

I cannot adequately describe the feeling, even to this day, but what I can describe was FPC-Beckley. Prison would be a relief. I was finally away from Martens and Britt.

CHAPTER 34

JAILHOUSE LAWYER

"The more laws, the less justice."

Marcus Tullius Cicero, 43 B.C.

February 8, 2008 – FPC-Beckley

I t was not until federal prison, when it was too late, that I was allowed to visit a law library for the first time. The night of arrival, I read the Speedy Trial Act in its entirety, and learned I was right. Had any attorney filed for dismissal of the indictment, as instructed in writing, it would have been dismissed in 2006 as a matter of law by any fair court, and I would not be in prison.

Day Two, I was in the law library at 6:30 a.m. and verified Kirk Osborn's citations. Rick Graves' acquittal had indeed acted to acquit me and voided the plea, as Kirk said, but somehow I was in federal prison instead of free. The case Kirk mentioned, was *United States v. Austin-Bagley Corp.*, 279 US 863, 73 LEd 1002, 49 S.Ct. 479; only slightly different from the name in my journal in 2007.

Austin-Bagley was the seminal case on this issue after the country passed its first expansion of *conspiracy* laws, and the Court ruled, "Acquittal of all defendants except one invalidated conviction of latter."

The other case he mentioned, *United States v. Musgrave*, 414 US 1025, 38 LEd2d 316, 94 S.Ct. 450, was listed in the annotated statute book itself, with the law, and said, "Conviction of only one defendant in conspiracy prosecution under 18 USCS §371 will not be upheld where all other alleged co-conspirators were acquitted." It could not be plainer, as 18 U.S.C. §371 was the statute under which I was falsely charged.

I lived in the law library and eventually became its librarian. By September, I had learned enough to file my own appeals and suits.

In those studies, I read of a major Native American victory in the Supreme Court by a Lakota Sioux prisoner. The court thereby awarded all Native American prisoners the right to hold their traditional sweat lodge ceremonies as a matter of religious freedom. Counselors and case managers tried their best to kill it at FPC-Beckley by not allowing incoming prisoners to sign in as Native American practitioners, just as Case Manager Smith did with me.

I filed a request to the chaplain to have my religious preference added into the record when Case Manager Smith refused. I attended two sweats, studying the native ways before coming to prison, and knew such practices would provide me something to hold onto. Case Manager Smith, Counselor Grimes and others were not going to prevent me from doing what the rules and law allowed.

I was officially recorded as a Native American in the federal records and given a blue identity card authorizing my participation in services. Counselor Grimes ordered me to lead a speaking class for prisoners (associated with Toastmasters International), an activity that conflicted in time with the sweat lodge ceremony. By then, Grimes and I had several confrontations, but this was the worst. I think he knew the weekly sweat lodge ceremony, though brutal, was my lifeline, and he was determined to make me lose it.

I ended the debate by saying, "Not even you are bold enough to mess with my religion and think you can get away with it, Mr. Grimes," and left.

In my experience, there are only two ways for prison officials to get in trouble: overt racism or religious intolerance. I have yet to find another act that might land them in trouble or in the court short of murder. Grimes yielded.

I filed the first appeal in my case that fall as a *habeas corpus* petition with the Southern District Court of West Virginia (*Howell W. Woltz v. United States of America*, 5:08-cv-1103). It was September, 2008. My petition claimed the Western District Court of charge and the Eastern District Court of adjudication were too biased to hear the review after what they had done in the underlying case, and therefore sought to have my conviction overturned by the court where I was held in West Virginia under *habeas corpus*. There were enough violations of law by Judge Britt and AUSA Martens to convince the court my sentence was illegal. Judge R. Clarke VanDervort responded within days:

"Having considered Plaintiff's claims in this matter and *circumstances apparent from the record of the proceedings in the Western District of North Carolina, the undersigned has concluded that this matter should be transferred to the Western District of North Carolina in the interest of justice pursuant* to 28 U.S.C. §1631.(p.1, ¶1). Because the Petitioner's claims in this matter appear to fall within the exceptions to his waivers [in the Plea Agreement], the undersigned finds that *Petitioner's* claims in this matter *would appear to be sufficiently meritorious and deserving consideration by the District Court with jurisdiction, the Western District of North Carolina, that the transfer of this matter there is in the interest of justice and therefore warranted*." (p.5, ¶2). (Emphasis added)

This was big. I was the happiest man in prison that day and considered packing up. I understood from others Judge VanDervort dismissed all *habeas* petitions filed from Beckley. Transfer to the Western District Court of jurisdiction "in the interest of justice," should preclude Judge Britt from touching it, another Federal court having found the misconduct "apparent from the record of the proceedings".

The new Chief Judge of the Western District, however, was former U.S. Attorney Robert J. Conrad, Jr. As the Western District U.S. Attorney, he bore responsibility for the tactics known to be used there, which were the same acts of "prosecutorial misconduct" outlined in the petition. Conrad was the U.S. Attorney who drew Chief Judge

Mullen's ire to the point of no longer accepting his plea bargains due to his unlawful and unconstitutional methods. My *habeas* petition was full of prosecutorial misconduct from the same office, a potential problem for now Chief Judge Conrad.

Another federal court had deemed the misconduct of his former office and the ineffectiveness of my lawyers as being *"apparent from the record."* I spent months trying to get others to listen and help redress the loss of foundational citizen rights without response. Judge VanDervort was the first impartial, dispassionate mind to review the case, and he saw those violations by reviewing the record on the docket sheet.

I concurrently filed a Motion to Vacate the Sentence pursuant to 28 U.S.C. §2255 in the Western District of North Carolina, challenging Judge Britt's constitutional authority to adjudicate a Western District case in his Eastern District Court, which should also make it a conflict for him to hear the appeal. AUSA Martens was challenged for his breach of contract, but absent a copy of the Non-Attribution Agreement, there was no proof. My own lawyers refused to provide it. I was hopeful Charlotte had it on file, and some objective person saw its importance to my wrongful conviction on the added charge.

At any rate, I was finally done with Judge W. Earl Britt. The appeal was docketed as Case No. 3:08-cv-438. I was almost home and knew it. Between the two appeals, relief had to be given as a matter of law.

The *habeas* petition forwarded by the West Virginia court was docketed in the Charlotte Division of the Western District of North Carolina as Case No. 3:08-cv-488. It must be decided there as a matter of law. When I received the court's response, however, it had been usurped by Judge Britt from his Eastern District court and re-characterized as a "successive 2255." Perhaps Judge Conrad allowed Britt to poach my *habeas* to avoid personal embarrassment, as it was he who had legal authority over my case, not Britt. It was his former office, however, that committed the prosecutorial misconduct recognized by the West Virginia federal court. Better to keep it out of sight and let Judge Britt dismiss it than have it out in the open where he presided, I can only presume. The case law Judge Britt cited, however, (*United States v. Emmanuel*, 288 F.3d 644 (2002)), forbid re-characterization unless I, the petitioner, agreed to it. That case stated:

"If, however, the movant responds within the time set by the court but does not agree to have the motion re-characterized, the court shall not treat it as a § 2255 motion but shall rule on the merits of the motion as filed."

My response was timely and filed under 28 U.S.C. §2241 (*habeas corpus*), not §2255 (Motion to Vacate Sentence). I challenged Judge Britt's lack of constitutional jurisdiction and due process. These were anything but technical challenges or matters of ineffective counsel. The §2241 nomenclature was to prevent a re-characterization by Britt. I knew a "successive 2255" would simply be dismissed without review. Although law required my petition to be heard *as filed* if I did not agree to its re-characterization, Judge Britt dismissed it on that basis in violation of the case law cited in his order.

I appealed to the Fourth Circuit and concurrently filed a complaint on Judge Britt's misconduct and lack of jurisdiction. The complaint included an affidavit regarding AUSA Martens' braggadocio about Judge Britt's bias and Martens' own orchestration of the appointment in favor of government. The Chief Judge of the Fourth Circuit, Karen Williams, agreed with the complaint language that characterized the "historical animus between Sam Currin and Judge Britt" in her response. Poaching the case of a public rival from another jurisdiction established the "appearance of impropriety," if not impropriety itself. Such actions would suggest punishment, if not removal as judge, under Judicial Canons I & II. Contrary to the Canons, however, Judge Williams argued that since the animus began long ago, it should not be considered. That did not comport with Canons I & II in the least, and what greater animus than one long held? Her ruling also failed to address the jurisdictional and constitutional issues or Britt's violations of federal law. In July, Judge Williams retired from the Fourth Circuit for reasons of health, the early stages of Alzheimer's disease. I appealed her ruling.

My complaint was dismissed, as were the next three. No court was willing to address Judge Britt's lack of jurisdiction or what I unflinchingly call his crimes.

It was then I read John Dean, former White House Counsel, and his on-going analysis of the federal judiciary. He was a recognized expert on the matter, having studied hundreds of complaints of judicial misconduct. Dean found only a handful of federal judges have been *impeached* in the nation's history, let alone removed, and none of the modern complaints he reviewed resulted in removal of the judge. This was particularly discouraging. My efforts felt like a waste of time; nonetheless, I filed multiple Motions to the Fourth Circuit for Writs of Mandamus seeking to have Judge Britt removed from the *case*, content to wait for others to remove him from the *bench*, but each was similarly dismissed without basis or reason.

A few weeks after filing the Motion to Vacate (§2255), I learned of a Supreme Court case in the BNA Criminal Law Reporter, *United States v. Santos*, which overturned my conviction on the money laundering allegation. The Supreme Court ruled that a defendant could only be sentenced based on "profits" rather than gross receipts. I was sentenced on the entire estimated and imaginary amount made up by government, and there were no profits. Our costs of carrying the trust exceeded fees for the brief time we held the investment prior to dismissing Sam and his clients over source of funds questions. In other words, we suffered a loss, not a gain. The ruling stated:

> *On collateral review, the District Court ruled that, under intervening Circuit precedent interpreting the word "proceeds" in the federal money-laundering statute, §1956(a)(1)(A)(i) applies only to transactions involving criminal profits, not criminal receipts. Finding no evidence that the transactions on which respondents' money-laundering convictions were based involved lottery profits, the court vacated those convictions. The Seventh Circuit affirmed.*
>
> *Held: The judgment is affirmed.*
>
> *461 F. 3d 886, affirmed.*

The Supreme Court used the normal economic definition of *profit,* which is *net proceeds over expenses.* The government had invented its own definition of "profits," preferring to use *gross proceeds* for the purpose of increasing the length of my sentence.

I never profited in any way from the trust assets we managed for Sam Currin or his clients, and unlike Santos, I never received any remuneration of any kind or salary from our trust company. What AUSA Martens called "money laundering" under definition of statute, had in fact been nothing more than a transfer from our trust company to another trustee, and we lost money doing so. The *Santos* ruling had not changed the law. The Supreme Court simply ruled that government had misused the statute, precisely as they had in my case.

There were so many reasons and opportunities to overturn my false imprisonment I lost count. The jury acquittal of Rick Graves acquitted me as well on the conspiracy charge. The Supreme Court decision in *Santos* acted to void the unlawfully added second charge that violated the Non-Attribution Agreement and thirty-day rule of 18 U.S.C. §3161(b), but finding an "honest" court was proving to be a Diogenian search like the earlier one for an honest man.

I immediately filed a request with the central librarian for the *Santos* case. It was not in the prison law library, though the case was decided the preceding year. I also filed a Motion to Amend my §2255, which was filed three weeks earlier. At that time, Civil Procedure Rule 15(a) allowed such an amendment "as a matter of course," so not even Judge Britt could deny it under the Rules of Procedure.

The central librarian refused my requests for the *Santos* case and Judge Britt and the Western District Clerk, "Johnsy", refused to file my amendment, though the Federal Rules of Civil Procedure required it. I filed the amendment a second time, and again they refused to file it. I sent a third copy to the appointed judge, David C. Keesler, who was assigned to my case and should have been hearing the appeal. Judge Keesler personally had the Clerk file the amendment. Judge Britt then dismissed the first two filings as "duplicative" as cover, I suppose, but refused to rule on the *Santos* amendment to my appeal. No court has yet addressed this issue including the U.S. Supreme Court.

Government missed its deadline for responding to the §2255 (Motion to Vacate) in October of 2008. Judge Britt gave Martens an extension, without his asking for it, while turning down my request for one during that same period. Judge Britt gave them a second, third, fourth, and fifth extension, all of which they also missed. By then it was February of 2009. Government's response was due no later than January 27 on the final extension. The envelope mail meter indicates the U.S. Attorney's Office posted it the following week on February 3 (I still have the envelope), but lied on their Certificate of Service to make the filing appear timely. I filed for Summary Judgment due to Government's failure to respond within the time limit.

Although the response was filed late and could not be used legally by the court, it was of great value to me. The basis for government's response was two affidavits against me, written by my own lawyers, David B. Freedman and Matthew J. Hoefling.

David Freedman's affidavit included twenty-one counts of material misstatements and perjury, but more importantly, it referenced the Non-Attribution Agreement both Hoefling and he had withheld. Until receiving his affidavit, I was unable to prove the Agreement existed. Freedman's affidavit was dated January 14, 2009, and stated:

"Before I allowed Mr. Woltz to talk to the Government, I had obtained a Non-Attribution Agreement from the prosecutors, which served as an immunity letter allowing Mr. Woltz to incriminate himself without repercussion."

Although Agent Schiller admitted I broke no law, "without repercussion" became eighty-seven months in federal prison a year later.

I filed a Motion to the Western District Court seeking Rule 11 Sanctions against David B. Freedman for filing false material statements under oath, and against government for lying on its certificate of service for an improper purpose. David was guilty of criminal perjury and the government attorney was guilty of suborning it, both federal crimes. There was also lying by government on a certificate of service, to make the response appear timely when it was not. My letter to the Office of the U.S. Attorney regarding these crimes was ignored.

Meanwhile, I filed a lawsuit against the two attorneys (Freedman and Hoefling) hoping, among other things, to force the return of my files via the *discovery process*, so I could get a copy of the Non-Attribution Agreement and prove the claims.

Freedman's attorneys scheduled a hearing for April 13, 2009 to dismiss my suit against him in state court, based on an affidavit not included in their motion. A letter arrived three working days before the hearing claiming the affidavit referenced in the dismissal motion was "inadvertently left out" acting to prevent me time for response. David's affidavit in the state court case contained fourteen counts of material perjury, and was tardily filed in that case as well. Although David refused to release my files proving his wrongdoing, Art Strickland, the former Federal Magistrate Judge, found copies of enough documents to prove fraud and perjury. I spent all night pulling together what evidence I had, such as the jailhouse visitation log and other case documents proving his affidavit false. Art had also found copies of my letters, which David claimed did not exist and forwarded them to me. He concurrently contacted the North Carolina State Bar, providing them substantial evidence regarding David's misrepresentations and lies. To my bemusement but not surprise, no action was taken by the State Bar against him then or since.

The Bar had enough evidence to establish beyond reasonable doubt David Freedman committed a fraud upon both the State and Federal courts in his affidavits, as well as material perjury, crimes at both levels, but made no referrals for prosecution or effort to punish him. The State Bar has acted to protect all these men instead.

On April 13, 2009 my packet of evidence was delivered to the court in Davie County, North Carolina, just minutes before the hearing began. Jim, who hired and paid David, sent an affidavit disputing his claims as well, which meant the judge could not dismiss the suit, as there were issues remaining "in controversy." Under Rule 56, (Summary Judgment), such issues must go to trial.

Since I was not allowed to be there, my dear friend and Chief of Police, Robert Cook, agreed to attend and be a witness. According to Robert, who had been a magistrate judge of twenty-five years before becoming Chief of Police, the Judge, Joseph N. Crosswhite, improperly discussed and handled the case with the attorneys for Lawyers Mutual representing David. Both took exception and otherwise ridiculed my efforts to sue an attorney in the State of North Carolina. Robert said the court ruling was predetermined. "It was as if they were discussing something that had already been ruled upon," he later wrote in affidavit.

The attorneys for David Freedman represented Lawyers Mutual Insurance Company. They were there to prevent a claim of malpractice, a potential financial penalty for which the company would be liable. Their open, cozy conversation with Judge Crosswhite troubled Robert.

The proceedings were held, not in a courtroom, but a small office. Our packets of evidence, including Jim's affidavit, were never opened. Both sat on the table in front of Judge Crosswhite throughout the proceeding. Their label, *priority mail*, did not make them so for Judge Crosswhite. Robert wrote the Judge a letter, one I recently found in the Clerk of Court's file while preparing the record on appeal. He provided an affidavit about Judge Crosswhite's impropriety, as well as his original letter to the court in later hearings in 2013, at which time my suit was dismissed. He wrote:

Dear Judge Crosswhite:

My name is Robert Cook, Chief of Police here in Mocksville. I believe you have met me only once, while you were holding a hearing on Woltz vs. Freedman.

Judge, in the past I have been Chief Deputy Sheriff for five years and Assistant Chief of Police in Kernersville five years. I am a retired magistrate of 25 years, and am currently starting my fifth year as Chief of Police in Mocksville, NC.

Judge, I have never gone to bat so hard for someone in my life, and have never wavered because Mr. Woltz has had his rights violated over and over. I am the person who took his kids out of their beds after they had been left by U.S. agents. I kept one child for one year until he finished high school, and was at almost every hearing Mr. Woltz had. He had no legal representation worth $15.00.

Your Honor, I was at that hearing (Woltz v. Freedman) with the intent to testify. I did not openly address the Court out of deep respect, but I did raise my hand to notify the Court I was a first-hand witness, but was ignored.

I wonder what would ever be the outcome if just the truth was on the table.

Sincerely,

Robert W. Cook, Chief of Police

Years later (April of 2013) I looked up the original Order of Dismissal at the Davie County courthouse and it was clear Robert's assessment was correct. Judge Crosswhite signed and dated the Order on April 8, 2009, five days *before* the hearing. The copy I received from the attorneys at Lawyers Mutual Insurance Company was undated and their Certificate of Service was without signature, indicating, in my opinion, they were knowledgeable and active participants in the fraud.

On April 16, 2009, just three days later, I was pulled from my job at General Maintenance and taken to the FCI. They stripped me, chained me, and shipped me to a county jail in Chickasha, Oklahoma, though to this day, no one has ever told me why.

CHAPTER 35

ON THE ROAD AGAIN

"Woe to those who decree unjust statutes and to those who continually record unjust decisions, to deprive the needy of justice, and to rob the poorest of My people of their rights..."

Isaiah 10:1.2

April 16, 2009 – FPC-Beckley to Grady County, Oklahoma

Counselor Grimes told me upon arrival in federal prison that we would not get along. He then made sure of it. He saw to it my small living space was torn up regularly and my job changed each time I "moved up the ladder." They saw the outcome of my legal self-training. As law librarian, other inmates were receiving some legal assistance, and I was in the law library all that time would allow working on my own appeals as well. Someone did not like it. I lost my job as law librarian and was put to the lowest, most menial tasks the prison had to offer, such as cleaning the shower drains and unclogging toilets.

Art Strickland, the attorney and former Federal Magistrate Judge, took an interest in my case and came to visit. On the first time, they sent him to the FCI, knowing I was not there and made him wait. Meanwhile, I was called to the Message Center and interrogated as to why an attorney had come to visit.

"Ask him," I replied.

Officer Michael Cutright liked any excuse to determine he had been treated impertinently. Off we went to the small prisoner shakedown room where he threw me against the concrete wall, applied a cross-neck chokehold, and struck me repeatedly.

"We don't like no motherfucking lawyers on this hill! You got that, Woltz? You better get rid of that son-of-a-bitch as quick as you can. You tell him one thing about what goes on up here and I'll have you sent to the hole and killed."

The shouting and beating continued for several minutes, but no matter how bad the abuse, a prisoner knows the consequences of fighting back.

By the time Art arrived from the FCI, I was pretty tousled. We had never met. I walked in the attorney meeting room and was greeted.

"What the hell happened to you?"

I talked and he wrote.

"I'll have you out of here tomorrow."

"No. I think I'm supposed to stay here and do something about this. Please make your notes so that if something happens to me, you will have a record, but just help me do something to change this place."

After Art left, Officer Cutright called me to the Message Center, and we had session two. I was against the wall in another chokehold. The yelling continued.

"Damn it, Cutright," Officer Jarrell shouted from behind, "this man is my responsibility! You'll get us both fired."

I was told to leave. Cutright found himself in someone else's grasp.

The abuse handed out to inmates took all forms. There was a complete absence of compassion in every area. I was not allowed dental treatment the entire time I was held by government, in spite of several requests, and arrived at FPC-Beckley with an abscessed tooth. The following year, it remained untreated, despite seventeen more requests. By then, the untreated infection caused a chronic sinus inflammation, which spread into the auditory canal on the right side of my head.

Counselor Grimes made sure medical help was not available. Nurse Conley White, a huge man, whose don't-mess-with-me attitude was his Harley Davidson skullcap, assaulted me for filing treatment requests. By the time Judge Britt put me on the road again in April of 2009, the pain was nearly unbearable.

Before shipping out Counselor Grimes warned I might soon be sent to Charlotte, NC "for your appeal." There had been no notification of a hearing, so I noted something was up. Any time I was to go on *diesel therapy*, special attention to my files was required. In this case, I kept the file for the §2255 appeal with me twenty-four hours a day. If there were to be a Charlotte hearing, as Grimes suggested, the files would have to be there too. On April 16 of 2009 they plucked me from my job, without warning, and took me to the FCI. I had the file with me.

I was taken by bus to Lewisburg, WV, and then to Oklahoma City on Prison Air Transport, trussed in chains, though I came from a camp without a fence.

After arriving in Oklahoma City via Memphis and Kansas City, I was put on another bus to the Grady County Jail in Chickasha, Oklahoma. For several days my new home was a twenty-foot shipping container with bunks and toilet mounted inside.

From Chickasha, a Motion was filed with the Western District Court demanding to know why I was shipped from federal prison. Days later, I was flown to upstate New York, then Philadelphia, then Atlanta.

I was again taken to USP-Atlanta, but this time, it was to a section added on to the original 1908 structure. From there, it was to the Mecklenburg County Jail in Charlotte and a return to the sleep deprivation pod. The request filed with the jail asked why I was there, as was my right to know. An administrator recognized my name and came to visit. She called Martens, asking for an explanation. I was "to be charged with more crimes," was the answer she relayed.

A large fight broke out the second night. Although not a combatant in the melee, I was caught in the crossfire, knocked into the air, and came down on my elbow. The fall pushed the humeral head of my right arm up through the rotator cuff, and it sat there on top of my shoulder like a baseball. The pain was excruciating and the injury was obvious, but treatment was denied. My family contacted Art Strickland, and he called the U.S. marshals. By 10 a.m. the next morning, I was on the way to the hospital. The guard pulled me out of the sheriff's car by my bad shoulder and handcuffs. The pain rifled though my body, and I inadvertently cried out.

An evangelist heard the scream and ran from across the street, waving his Bible, shaking it like he was going to hit me.

"Repent. Repent"

He like others saw only sins and crimes. Did he also see hypocrisy? Almost every man he worshipped in that book, from St. John of Patmos to Jesus of Nazareth, was also a prisoner.

Once inside the Carolinas Medical Center, the technician, upon examining the X-ray, said my shoulder was seriously dislocated and torn. I then waited for the doctor who treated patients from the jail. His name badge said "Dr. Krishnaraj."

"This guy is a *prisoner,*" the guard told him. "You understand, Doc? A *prisoner.*"

Dr. Krishnaraj grabbed my arm without elaboration or comment, jerked the humeral head back down even with the socket, and began walking out of the room. I was about to pass out from pain, but called after him. He stopped, turned around, came back into the room, gave me one ibuprofen in a paper cup, pulled a navy blue sling out of a drawer and threw it in my direction. This time he did leave, having never said a word.

I couldn't sleep or get up and down from the floor without assistance. I filed daily complaints to be moved. Either by accident or intent, I was moved to the familiar, murderer's pod, 6800, my home for most of the seventeen month pre-trial period. As incredible as it seemed, some of the men from those years were still there, awaiting trial.

I filed grievance forms and medical requests for help with the abscessed tooth and broken shoulder. Art got involved again, and I was taken to the Carolinas Medical Center for an MRI. Dr. Healy told the prison doctor, by videoconference and in my presence, I would never have full use of the right arm again without surgery. He said the humeral head was cracked; the supra and infra spinatus muscles were torn and must be re-attached; and the labrum, which acts as the joint's lining, had been ripped apart, out of the socket. I never got any treatment for the shoulder then or during the remaining years in prison, though the prison surgeon gave the same report and recommendation when I was returned to FPC-Beckley months later.

Before leaving prison on the unexpected "road trip," I filed a lawsuit against the McGuire Woods attorneys in the federal court in West Virginia. The same Judge, R. Clarke VanDervort, who ruled positively in the *habeas* petition, ruled, since both parties were from the same *state*, I did not have "diversity of jurisdiction" to sue them in *federal* court. McGuire Woods then pre-emptively sued me for bills erroneously submitted months *after* they were fired, though they were paid in full up to date of termination. Their action was filed in Charlotte where their power is great and their friends are influential. I would thus be prevented from filing an action in a more neutral court.

They had the audacity to submit bills after their termination as high as $10,000 each. The justification and authorization for work and hours and expenses did not exist. I counterclaimed and sued for malpractice, negligence and fraud.

McGuire Woods' soaking through Mayberry and Hoefling topped one-quarter million dollars. Three other attorneys had worked on my behalf, Tolly, Jack, and Kirk. They did so upon my request. The McGuire Woods attorneys, however, had ultimately entered the equation under false order of Judge Britt. This made for a fundamental difference in our relationships. It proved to be a costly difference as well, one to my financial detriment for sure, but one that more importantly increased the probability I would also pay an undue debt to society, in the form of lost years. That debt too should never have been paid.

Despite their influence in Charlotte, I firmly believed a court existed that would fairly hear my case of negligence and fraud against McGuire Woods. The proceedings to come would suggest something different.

CHAPTER 36

THE LAWYERS GUILD

"Resistance to tyrants is obedience to God."

Thomas Jefferson

April-August, 2009 – Mecklenburg County Jail, Charlotte, NC

Between the abscessed tooth pain and the broken shoulder, sleep was impossible until exhaustion overtook me each night. I would daydream and find myself in the sweat lodge, singing beautiful Lakota songs. "Grandfathers," the heated stones, showed orange bright. The dark *inipi* eased the pain.

Native traditions tell the circle of life. Each May brings destruction followed by rebuilding. For us, twenty-one saplings were cut and dropped off at our little sacred grounds by the Landscaping crew, which I missed that year. We were given one day off from work to bend thin branches over and twist them to create a new dome. Mother Earth's womb took form.

The dome was covered with army blankets and a tarp, leaving the womb dark. The 'grandfathers' were illuminated by a sacred fire made from downed trees gathered by Landscaping.

The ceremony is comprised of four *doors* or parts, each in honor of a direction of the Four Winds. Seven or more stones are brought in at each door, and the flap facing East closed. An Elder of the Circle leads each week's ceremony. The first door welcomes the spirits. The second is to give prayer for others, not ourselves. The third is for giving thanks for all of The Creator's blessings. The fourth is for sending back the spirits, with our thanks and prayers.

The ceremonies allowed me to magically escape hours of Mecklenburg pain. I felt my spirit being restored.

Writing also kept my mind off the pain. With ample paper and pencils in the appeal file, I set up shop in pod 6800 and worked on speedy trial dismissal motions for the men held there in violation of that Act. Almost all were many months beyond their seventy-day limit. Some had waited for years. It was as if Chief Judge Conrad ignored the existence of the federal statute.

Their particular refusal to allow access to the law library in Charlotte required a means of circumvention. Most important was case law and the Rules of Procedure in filings other than Speedy Trial, which I had more or less memorized. I would call my mother, Pat, and she would call Ms. Delores Hannah in Beckley, West Virginia, who was the mother of the law librarian at the Camp. Ms. Hannah asked Edmond Hannah to research what was needed. He in turn mailed it to the jail. We jokingly called our little coterie of jailhouse advocates *the Lawyers Guild*, and we succeeded, courtesy of another branch of the same government that was denying our rights in Charlotte.

I taught anyone who wanted to learn how to file motions and suits. We started filing them every day and getting results. It was exciting. Lawyers, whom many of these men had not seen for years, began coming regularly after being chastised by the federal judges in Charlotte for their clients filing for dismissal.

Next, we filed a federal lawsuit against the past and present Sheriffs of Mecklenburg County for not allowing us access to the law library. Within days, requests were granted. In 2006 and 2007 I was denied access during the critical pre-trial phase, otherwise, our fate may have been different. I did not want that happening to others.

We then filed a joint action over the denial of medical and dental care, which brought results. While my tooth was not pulled immediately, I was put on the schedule to have it done. All requests for dental care during pre-trial had been ignored.

Soon thereafter, a deputy sheriff attempted to serve me papers from McGuire Woods' attorney, Stephen M. Russell, Sr. He represented Lawyers Mutual Insurance Company for Matt Hoefling and Bill Mayberry in my counterclaim for malpractice and fraud. The officer said he claimed to represent *me* in order to gain access to serve me papers. I told the deputy that was untrue, and he should be reported for it. He came again, but I refused to accept them without proper service.

A few days later, I was taken to the Sergeant's office and put before a speakerphone. I was told it was a hearing, though any hearing requires notice to all parties. McGuire Woods had refused to answer any of my interrogatories or engage in the discovery process in my suit, and the court refused to force them. On the other hand I was being ordered deposed outside of due process by a Mecklenburg County judge who would not give his name at an unnoticed telephonic hearing. I was being written in to a Kafka play.

The judge ordered me to be deposed in spite of my objections and his lack of due process. I appealed on the spot, pointing out the lawlessness of the proceeding and filed a complaint with the Judicial Standards Commission of North Carolina that night. The next day, however, I was taken downstairs and deposed anyway, though I appealed the nameless judge's decision and it had not yet been heard. Attorney Russell was there with Bill Mayberry, a court reporter, and a video camera. I refused to be filmed in a prison outfit, court order or not, and they could not make me, but I had to comply with the order for deposition, or be held in contempt of court. A copy of the order was requested; it would have the nameless judge's signature on it. This was the only way to find who he was. It was added to my judicial complaint and sent out that night.

Paul K. Ross of the Judicial Standards Commission filed my complaint, but the committee ruled that while it did not condone the judge's misconduct, they chose not to sanction or punish him. This was the same game I experienced at the federal level. It is extremely difficult to have a judge sanctioned or removed, even for egregious misconduct. It is easier to raise attention for a petty public embarrassment than for a violation of citizens' rights, Judicial Canons or law. John Dean must have done his research in North Carolina.

The deposition was a flop for them. Bill Mayberry became so flummoxed by my answers, he stormed out at one point. Attorney Russell asked the court reporter, Shannon Colangelo, to turn off the microphone while Mayberry was gone, and inquired, "Did they really do all of that?"

"Yes. All of it."

He just shook his head in disbelief, though his own tactics on their behalf were little better.

These bizarre hearings and depositions with McGuire Woods were the only activities during those months on the road. I was removed from Beckley and sent on that long trip for no known purpose. Later I would learn of Judge Britt's role. As to *why* he ordered me taken on the lengthy, expensive "joy ride," he never replied. I am unsure if McGuire Woods or Lawyers Mutual Insurance Company worked in concert with Britt, but the form of the hearings and depositions certainly worked to their unfair advantage and my detriment.

Meanwhile, the Lawyer's Guild in pod 6800 was causing a stir. We filed so many motions for dismissal of federal indictments under the Speedy Trial Act that former U.S. Attorney, now federal Judge, Frank D. Whitney, shut down his court for a day. He was angry because *we* found out what *they* were doing was unlawful. Whitney ordered into his court those who practiced before him to determine who had discussed the Speedy Trial Act with his or her clients. One of those attorneys had the courage to share this with us.

I was mystified by Judge Whitney's indignation. *Thousands* were or had been unlawfully held in his judicial district. What right had *he* to be outraged by prisoners who had the temerity to ask him for a speedy trial, to not be held in perpetuity, and have their constitutional rights protected, as was his duty? I came to the conclusion that no prosecutor should ever be allowed to become a judge. Putting a black robe on them covered their stripes but did not remove them. They remained prosecutors.

We also began filing complaints with the U.S. marshals over the jail's failure to meet dietary standards, address overcrowding, curb abusive guards, provide medical care, and provide due process in the jail's grievance procedures. The jail came under intense scrutiny.

About that same time, Judge Whitney found out I was the source of the Speedy Trial information. I inadvertently signed my name to a Motion for Dismissal to his court for a prisoner, Sanchez Hudson, who was being illegally held. By late August, my welcome was apparently worn out and I was taken by bus to a private prison in Ocilla, Georgia known as the Irwin County Detention Center. A day later U.S. marshals descended on Mecklenburg. A letter from a fellow prisoner suggested the Sheriff and guards blamed me for their trouble.

CHAPTER 37

A MOVEABLE FEAST

"Whatever the human law may be, neither an individual nor a nation can commit the least act of injustice against the obscurest individual without having to pay a penalty for it."

Henry David Thoreau, 1862

August 18, 2009 – Irwin County Detention Center, Ocilla, Georgia

Having been moved from Charlotte, it reasoned Counselor Grimes misled me about being sent there for a hearing on the §2255 appeal. Fortunately, AUSA Martens was also less-than-truthful about having me face more charges. I never heard of someone serving a sentence being pulled out of prison for a joy ride around the country unless he or she were going back to trial or to testify for government. Something improper was brewing, I just didn't know what. It lasted five months, and included two trips around the country on jets, buses, and vans, all at taxpayer expense, for no discernable purpose other than to deprive me of constitutional rights, ones retained, even as a prisoner. There were no appearances in courtrooms and no official actions other than improper interface with McGuire Woods' attorneys, but at each stop, I plied the trade of jailhouse lawyer and assisted others. Once pencil, paper and envelopes were in hand, we were in business filing motions and teaching others how to do it. It was a moveable feast.

The next stop, Irwin County Detention Center, was in the middle of cotton country on the Florida border, and I did not like it or want more 'vacation'. Unfortunately, they pulled me out of Mecklenburg just three days before the abscessed tooth was to be pulled. Between the shoulder and tooth, I was miserable. My food tray was exchanged for a stamp and an envelope that first night in Ocilla, GA and I used the back of an Inmate Handbook cover to write a *habeas* petition requesting the reason for the detention in Ocilla and to be returned to Federal prison absent one. It was immediately filed by the West Virginia federal court as Case No. 5:09-cv-932 and forwarded to the Middle District of Georgia where it became Case No. 7:09-cv-104. The new warden called me three days later. She was a stumpy, elderly lady, about 5'2". She walked around me twice and said, "This is my first day on the job here, Woltz, and I got served papers by U.S. marshals because of you. That does not make me happy."

I was out of there in an hour and back in Beaver, West Virginia within a week via Grady County, Oklahoma and Prison Air Transport.

The first person I saw upon entering Evergreen Unit was Counselor John Grimes. He held out his hands and said, "What the fuck, Dog! How the hell did you get back here? They were supposed to ride you around until Christmas."

That confirmed it. Some vindictive combination of miscreants wanted me away from the law library and planned to keep me out of it all year on *diesel therapy*.

I left the perplexed Grimes, headed to the sweat lodge, and gave thanks for being returned. It was Wednesday and the ceremony was still in progress. Missing from the scene were the fire keepers, the eyes and ears of those inside.

The door flap opened and when the steam cleared, there were only four brothers. I knew immediately Beckley's management had tried to destroy our Circle.

This meant it must be rebuilt and protected. A suit against the warden, camp administrator, and captain of the guards ensured the right to hold services. I studied the native ways with a passion, and though being a white man, eventually became a Circle Elder and found myself teaching native ways to Native Americans. We rebuilt the Circle, thanks to devoted native brothers who had transferred to Beckley. By 2012 it was stronger than ever.

In my absence, Art Strickland obtained many of my files from both Freedman and McGuire Woods on order of the N.C. State Bar, but exclusive of the Non-Attribution Agreement. These documents formed the basis of a 110-page addendum to the motion filed for sanctions while on diesel therapy and established my claims of perjury in Freedman's affidavit. His statements were extraordinary. The jailhouse logs refuted sworn claims of his visits, and the correspondence from his own files directly disputed several other statements made under penalty of perjury, twenty-one in total. It was clear he never expected me to get these files. Art Strickland's fine legwork convinced the State Bar to act, but even on its order, none of these attorneys would give up the Non-Attribution Agreement, the document that best precluded my being in prison. My lengthy brief also established both firms' negligence and malpractice. How else can one characterize such actions that allowed a man to go to prison in violation of a contract and outside of law? I later confirmed this was the reason the Non-Attribution Agreement was not released until years later when the statute of limitations ran out. In North Carolina, special protections are afforded attorneys under N.C. General Statute 1-15(C), and if they can prevent turning over records proving their malpractice for 48 months, they escape suit, under law. But Britt once again poached my motion from the Western District and summarily dismissed it without the requisite hearing or review, claiming in his order that no evidence against Freedman or government had been provided. The damning evidence was unacknowledged by Judge Britt, though of record in the case. My Motion for Discovery, to get the evidence from Freedman, was denied by Judge Britt as well.

Upon return I also filed a suit against the warden and medical staff for physical abuse of inmates and failing to provide medical attention for my abscessed tooth for seventeen months. Counselor Grimes said I would *never* see the dentist. Three days later, the dentist pulled my tooth. After that, Grimes said they would put me "on the road again," if I ever filed another suit.

"If you people are going to hold me here illegally, Mr. Grimes, then I'm going to make sure all of you follow the law while I'm here." I departed, not waiting for a reply.

Following that conversation, I filed a suit against Camp Administrator Scarantino, his secretary, Laura Trump; Counselor Grimes, and Case Manager Smith for mail tampering. My outbound court and legal mail were being opened, which was forbidden by the Code of Federal Regulations and law, and my inbound legal mail, something permitted to be opened only in my presence to check for contraband, was regularly cut open. What they were doing was not only in violation of their own rules, but a federal crime.

I also sued the Counselors and Case managers, including Grimes, for falsifying records to prevent prisoners from being released on time. As pay clerk at General Maintenance, I found out what they were doing and brought the fraud to the attention of my boss, Tom Marabillas. He and another decent officer, Mr. Sherwood, took the findings to the warden. Warden Ziegler refused to address the issue (and chastised these two men for bringing the information to his attention), so I had little choice but to file a suit against them all, with Counselor Grimes as lead defendant.

As pay clerk I was allowed access to proof of the crime. Marabillas and Sherwood's monthly reports for each man showed more favorable ratings then those in the semi-annual prisoner evaluations prepared by the counselors and case managers, which acted as the official record. "Good" or better work ratings meant a lower security status and release to home confinement for the last six months of sentence. Less than "good" caused men to lose that opportunity, acting to keep them in prison or at a halfway house longer than they should have under law.

Large prison populations ensure large prison staffs. There exists a perverse reason why the union prison workforce would institutionalize the falsification of prisoner records: job security. Six months before a prisoner's *out date* there is also a mandatory status change to *community custody*. The officials at Beckley ignored this statutory provision and extended prison sentences with false or unfair work records. I never saw a person receive the mandatory opportunity for six months of home confinement, and while I cannot prove it, I have a reasonable suspicion that former shop steward Grimes was the scheme's instigator and ringleader.

Although the additional prison time may have acted to bolster job security for the guards and counselors, it cost the U.S. government a great deal of money. I filed the suit on *behalf* of the United States as allowed under the False Claims Act, calculating this fraud to have cost in excess of fifty million dollars since my arrival, by multiplying the prison population turnover rate by the published annual cost of incarceration. The courts had no idea what to make of this case. A federal prisoner had never before filed a False Claims Act suit on behalf of the federal government, to protect it from criminal activity by its own employees. It seemed to cause quite a stir.

Art made sure the defendants were served summonses during their workday so all could see. The Court had no choice but to docket the case. Bells rang in Beckley and in Washington, D.C.; the Office of the Attorney General made a responsive filing.

I had further endeared myself to Grimes. He and his crew retaliated by putting a man with communicable hepatitis C in my two-person cell. Medical refused to give him *interferon*, which would have lessened or eliminated the disease's communicability, but was expensive. I soon tired of cleaning up John's diarrhea and getting him new clothes from laundry each week as the prisoner employees refused to wash his soiled clothing with their own and others. John was also crippled and could do very little for himself. A hunger strike on his behalf was the best way to help him while protecting the population at-large and myself. The assistant warden and camp administrator came to our cell the third night stating they would not tolerate a hunger strike, and claimed I was "inciting a riot." They threatened to charge me with that infraction and send me to the Segregated Housing Unit (SHU) at the FCI as punishment. The claim was frivolous, as I had informed only the warden of my actions, by letter, but no other prisoners or staff. The test of wills fell in my favor and that of "Little John"; he began treatment the next day, and I resumed eating.

The opportunities and reasons to file suits went unabated. I filed one against the prison officials after the 2010 U.S. Census. Grimes ordered our unit to leave "place of residence" blank on the census form, though the official instruction given by the warden required each prisoner to put his or her home address if one existed. Those who supplied their home address were reprimanded, and had the *error* corrected by the unit staff. Counselor Grimes and the other officers put "Beaver, WV" on the forms. This fraud acted to re-channel approximately twenty thousand dollars of federal funding per inmate to Beaver, West Virginia rather than the men's home communities. Worse, this miscalculation distorted the voting district population, giving West Virginia disproportionate representation. Given the number of people incarcerated in the country, the impact of such misrepresentation can decisively change a political map.

My ongoing advocacy of this sort served to sharpen the attention I received from Grimes and crew. Deprivations were incessant and mistreatments severe at times. I was taunted, mugged, threatened, and generally assaulted. My person and cell were subject to regular shakedowns. Anything and everything was done to curtail filings, including tampering with records filed by other officers. Mrs. Fletcher of the Education Department filed records on my behalf, only to have them altered by Grimes. To her credit, she reported him to the legal staff, but if Grimes were slowed down, it was barely noticeable.

While these suits against the prison's bad actors had collateral effect, such actions are rarely successful in federal court because law (42 U.S.C. §1997e) requires all administrative remedies to be *exhausted* before a suit can be heard in federal court. The process is short-circuited by prison staff refusing to provide prisoners with required forms or removing filed complaints from the U.S. Mail, thereby destroying the process itself. FPC-Beckley regularly employed both methods.

In my judgment, filing a federal suit was the only way to bring attention to criminal conduct by prison officials to those outside Bureau of Prisons, even one destined for dismissal because the process was, in essence, inexhaustible. With a federal lawsuit, it became a matter of public record, and a scrutinizing investigation might occur.

One such suit was filed against the trustee of the Inmate Trust Fund, Thomas Clifton, and the warden for misuse of the Fund. Profits from the expensive phone system, over-priced Commissary, and other profit centers were required by law to accrue for the benefit of inmates. Prison officials, for their personal benefit, were illegally diverting the funds. Examples included lavish parties by the guards replete with well-known bands, held at the Training Center on weekends. The inmates, the ones who cleaned up the mess, knew the extent of the gatherings. An event's trash went to The Recycling Department and would include dozens of half-gallon whiskey bottles and a near truckload of beer cans. The cleaning crews often found ladies' underwear, used condoms, and drug paraphernalia as well. Items built for these parties included a large palm tree and a full-size metal replica of an alligator for just one tropical-themed party. These things remain in the General Maintenance yard. One staff member stepped forward to say she took exception to the parties and was upset to know the bashes were illegally paid for by the Inmate Trust Fund. This went a long way toward explaining why the Fund could not afford basic recreational items for the Camp. We estimated millions disappeared or were misapplied after being supplied with the figures on profits generated in the various feeders to the Inmate Trust Fund by inmates who worked in those areas.

The local court seemed to tire of allegations of the crimes and misbehavior. Prison officials were moved. The secretary to the Camp Administrator was transferred to another prison. She had taken my first grievance form from the U.S. Mail, held it until untimely, only to return it with a threatening note, and thus unknowingly gave me a tangible piece of evidence by which to file suit. She was transferred. The Camp Administrator, Thomas Scarantino, who encouraged or suborned this, was moved to a prison on the docks of Los Angeles, widely considered the worst post in the Bureau. Michael Cutright was forced to retire and soon thereafter suffered a heart attack. Nurse Conley White, rather than being fired or imprisoned for his assaults, was transferred to the VA Hospital. That was not enough. I successfully had his credentials suspended indefinitely with the West Virginia Board of Examiners for Registered Professional Nurses by providing them with over thirty sworn affidavits of his attacks on, and negligence of, prisoners under his care and custody. One incident involved an inmate death. Case Manager Smith and the rest of Grimes' crew were moved to the Medium FCI, where it was truly dangerous. And Trustee Thomas Clifton, rather than risk pension loss, took retirement. None were pleased with the threat of legal action but least so was Counselor John Grimes. He called me into his office one day in April of 2011.

"Motherfucker, you ain't got *me* off this mountain yet."

"The fact that you called me in here to tell me that, Mr. Grimes, lets me know I'm getting close. Thank you."

Grimes, to my knowledge, had physically assaulted three men in the preceding six months. I knew of them because I filed complaints on their behalf. Homemade complaint forms were used to notify The Bureau of Prisons. They were sent via family members and attorneys, bypassing the mail-tampering system. One assault was against 70-year old "Pop" Saunders, a gentleman of a person. Grimes destroyed his property and assaulted him in retaliation for seeking my assistance. The counselor kicked Pop Saunders so severely medical attention was required. We filed another complaint, directly to the Bureau of Prisons, as well as a lawsuit in federal Court. Grimes' wrath increased.

Pop Saunders' first cousin, Dr. Howell, was married to West Virginia's first black or female federal Judge, Irene C. Berger, who had recently been appointed by President Obama and confirmed by the U.S. Senate. Judge Berger took over all the suits and complaints against prison staff and management shortly after her appointment to the Southern West Virginia District. She was responsive. We were heard at last.

The case against Grimes was witnessed and well documented. He was caught emptying the U.S. Mail depository and going through it on numerous occasions. He was seen removing complaints, affidavits and legal filings to Judge Berger's court. He refused requests for grievance forms and threatened or assaulted those who asked for them. He committed census fraud and falsified government records. Each of these acts was cause for dismissal, crimes justifying prison, but the Bureau of Prisons refused to act.

In my observation punishment for internal wrongdoing or violation of B.O.P. policy is rare. Offenders are simply shuffled around until they retire. Judge Irene C. Berger, however, did not appear to be concerned with their internal policy.

Within three weeks of the Pop Saunders' court report, Counselor John Grimes, union shop steward and the most egregious abuser of prisoners and their rights, was shuffled off the hill and returned to the same housing unit at the FCI, where seven years before he was nearly killed by inmates. In addition to his departure, twenty-seven various guards, counselors, case managers, and officials named in these suits were transferred, forced to retire, or were punished by 2012. In the immediate years prior not a single personnel change had taken place at the Camp.

Perhaps the biggest stir occurred when Captain Jeremy Nash put the Camp on lock down. He hoped to stop the spate of inmate filings, which were showing the outside world the grimy reality of his institution and its personnel. Bureau of Prison rules forbade Camp lock downs, and we had never heard of one. Nash shut down everything, including the law library, Education Department, and Recreation. Except for work or meals, we were held inside the housing units.

Violence spiked as expected but the Nash decision was not reversed. The new Camp Administrator, Briggette Seafus, would not take action. The only person at FPC-Beckley who consistently followed Bureau policy was its Director of Education, Barbara Fletcher. I asked her for a typewriter to complete legal work during the lock-down, as policy required. Ms. Fletcher provided one despite the obvious risks this created for her. Each day after work and before the lock down, I checked a typewriter out of her office.

This lasted a total of eighty-three days between 2010 and 2011. When I finished drawing the lawsuit, the local federal court filed it but refused to issue summonses to the Defendants, Warden Ziegler, Captain Nash, and Camp Administrator Seafus. I mailed a copy to Art Strickland's office disguised under another prisoner's name to avoid drawing attention to it in the U.S. Mail box. Art's office drew the summonses and sent them to the Clerk of Court in Beckley to execute. He also hired a process server to deliver them directly to prison officials. Art knew what was going on in Beckley, and promised to help stop it. He and his legal assistant, Patty Ballard, were critical to the success of our many legal actions as most would not have been filed without their assistance. At the risk of sounding melodramatic, I believe they made it possible for me to survive Beckley because officials there knew Art, a former federal judge, was my eye and advocate watching my back.

When Washington examiners came on February 12, 2011 to investigate the lawsuit's allegations, staff was participating in an annual review at the Training Center. Administrators claimed the Camp had never been on lock down, though it was at the time and had been for almost seventy days. Ms. Fletcher, upon hearing her superiors say my allegations were untrue, told a different story. She had received written orders from administrators to lock down Education and the law library. My suit included copies of these same documents, but it was her testimony, which gave credence to accept as true the suit's claims.

Barbara Fletcher's courage and honesty were rewarded with sanctions. She was punished and transferred from the Camp to the infamous FCI. Her accomplishments at Beckley included setting the national standard for rate of GED graduations. I saw her months later and acknowledged her honesty in support of my allegations caused her punishment.

"Woltz," she said, "we did the right thing. We told the truth. The rest is God's will."

By the time the warden received his summons from Art's office, he was away at a conference in California. The Assistant Warden announced we were going on "total lock down" the day he returned. This included suspension of most jobs, closing of commissary, and elimination of religious services, all of which were illegal. Native brother, former Army Special Ops Officer James Holley, was the warden's orderly that day. He provided a first-hand account of what followed.

Warden Ziegler never cursed according to James.

"Holley, where is Captain Nash?"

"He just went in his office, Sir."

"Captain Nash! Get your ass out here now!"

Nash immediately offered a "Yes Sir."

"Captain Nash. I want you to get over to my goddamn Camp, and open it up right this minute!"

"Sir, we're going to do that eventually, but we want to do it in phases," Captain Nash replied.

"Captain Nash, you are not listening to me! I said for you to get your ass over to my fucking Camp, and open it right now! I just got a $10 million lawsuit because of you! Do you hear me Nash?"

Within fifteen minutes, Nash and the Assistant Warden were at the housing units announcing the change. The Camp was back to normal. Nash was unceremoniously transferred days later to the violent Philadelphia Detention Center.

By 2011, the lawsuits were all but over. The outstandingly bad guys were gone. Prison officials began hiring better personnel for the most part. Grimes' replacement, Timothy Painter, did not adopt his notorious leadership style. He was a decent man who did his job fairly. Even the Grimes-era leftovers behaved better, and many of them expressed their appreciation for the changes. Life became more pleasant and positive for both guards and prisoners. This happened despite persistent inaction by the local federal court, at least officially. Eventually all the suits were dismissed once I was released, nonetheless these actions brought to the Court's attention criminal conduct by prison officials. Collectively they caused profound change. That made my experience, no matter how painful, somewhat meaningful.

Unfortunately, Congress passed 18 U.S.C. §3626 **Appropriate remedies with respect to prison conditions.** The law provides protection for Bureau of Prisons and its union staff should anyone exhaust the dubious "administrative remedy process". Relief "shall extend no further than necessary to correct the violation of *the Federal right of a particular plaintiff or plaintiffs.*" Any relief must be "narrowly drawn, extend no further than necessary to correct the violation of the Federal right, and is the least intrusive means necessary to correct the violation of the Federal right." Prison reform is highly unlikely as long as those who suffer abuses are blocked from meaningful access to the federal courts or required to "exhaust" administrative remedies that do not functionally exist. And prison abuses will continue if those who commit the inhumanities are provided institutional protection, both from within and from without. While the larger justice system works to protect its own, it is the incarcerated that are twice penalized.

It is an ongoing battle for all prisoners to secure fair conditions and receive decent treatment from those who hold ultimate control over their lives. I for one received some late considerations from Timothy Painter. Upon request, my prison file was turned over, a stark contrast to denials by Grimes, though an acknowledged right. In reviewing it, I learned no writ was filed to take me out of prison back in 2009 for the extended joy ride around the nation. Judge Britt created the writ only after I filed a motion to the Western District Court asking for the purpose of my removal. Britt's order was signed and dated nine days *after* I was taken from prison. No purpose was stated.

Mr. Painter called me to his office a few days later. He told me to name the job I wanted. I replied, "Evening Compound Orderly."

"There is no such thing as an 'Evening Compound Orderly,' Woltz. You guys are locked in at night."

I repeated, "Evening Compound Orderly."

Mr. Painter typed the new job assignment into the computer, repeating "Evening Compound Orderly."

The rest of my Beckley days were calm with few exceptions. I took up running with accomplished marathoner, Charlie Engle; caught up on filing appeals, including one for him; and began writing a new book. By June, *The Way Back to America: A 10-step Plan to Restore the United States to Constitutional Government* was on Amazon. On one of those days Charlie and I completed 40 miles around the track in peace.

CHAPTER 38

THE HOME FRONT

"Law is a bottomless pit, it is a Cormorant, a Harpy that devours everything."

John Arbuthnot, 1735

January 7, 2011 – FPC-Beckley, West Virginia

Five prison years fray family ties. Relations with children grow distant, not from lack of love in either direction, but simply because the base of shared experiences is frozen in time. Visits could be strange for us both. We had little in common except a recent but distant past. I had not seen a movie, heard a new song, or watched TV (by choice) for over half a decade. I knew nothing about the popular culture in which they lived and read only *The Economist* and *The Guardian Weekly*, both British publications. There is little about prison life anyone wants to hear, and the stories unintentionally spoke of an absent father. We tried to act like things were normal, but it was rather clear they weren't. I would remain in prison uniform, and they were free to leave, without me. My daughter, according to her mother, quit coming altogether in later years because she cried both ways in anticipation of, and after seeing me, in a prison uniform.

On November 8, 2010, a visit occurred on my birthday. Vernice announced she was filing for divorce. After she left I walked for miles on the track. Those wonderful Bahamian days of 2006 were not on view.

By the following year, one particular January 7 was special, for my son John was coming to see me on *his* birthday.

We seemed to connect more or less as we did when he was twelve, before this all began, only now he was six feet tall and driving a car. He wanted to come see me, and we were both thrilled. We caught up on his life. For once I did not feel so isolated.

Vernice still came to visit on occasion despite the divorce filing and sent money from my personal funds to the commissary account each month. Our assets, including the company's capital accounts, were under our joint control, but tied up in long-term investments in other countries or rendered insolvent due to the market crash in 2008.

Our lives were bound by our children and our clients' capital accounts, which after my release would have to be retrieved and distributed. She came again during the summer of 2011, perhaps because of these interests, to tell me she had changed her mind. She did *not* want a divorce after all, though the documents were filed. The uncertainty was confusing.

This would clear after another November 8 visit the following year. She was moving ahead with her divorce filing in court after all. I came to terms with it but only after asking that her visits occur on someone else's birthday.

She requested I sign over authority of our personal and client funds to her friend and attorney, Carole Folmar, whom I have never known or met.

"No. That's not happening," I simply said. The visit ended.

Her request for my permission was after-the-fact. In February of 2013 an investigator determined she had placed my corporate capital accounts under the control of her Trinidad relations and the attorney falsely verified my presence and acquiescence to that act according to documents in my lawyer's possession. I would leave prison penniless but did not yet know it.

Mail dated "November 8" came the following week. Judge Britt denied my Motion to Vacate (§2255 Appeal) three years after its filing based solely on government's time-barred response and my own attorneys' perjured affidavits. I decided to quit having birthdays and stay 58 forever.

A few months later, Vernice and I spoke on the phone. She claimed to have changed her mind yet again. She did *not* want a divorce after all. Not yet knowing of her financial infidelity, I took hope.

I was able to survive years in prison by distancing myself from anything on the outside about which nothing could be done. That was more or less everything, but it is a hard task when it comes to family. Such emotional uncertainty is difficult to keep at a distance. I asked Vernice to make up her mind, for I needed finality. She committed to staying married, but I now suspect for reasons other than love.

Life after prison only held expectations of toil and a small income as an author. Two of my books related to, or the result of, the prison experience were published, which was a start. A film student at Savannah College of Art & Design asked and would go on to make a documentary based on the first version of *Justice Denied*. Through filing appeals I was able to help free a few men or have their sentences substantially reduced. Word spread through the prison community regarding the suits against prison officials, some of which were posted online and in the prison system computer for law libraries. With almost every nightly mail call I received something that resembled "fan mail." New prisoners from the Oklahoma City Transfer Center would tell stories, sometimes inaccurately, about what I had done. I was flattered just the same. Jailhouse lawyers in other prisons were supposedly copying my work. The system had to change, and it felt good to be a part of that effort. My future, married or not, was being pulled by the forces, actions and outcomes, that grew from an intent to help others and to secure some semblance of justice for my associates and myself.

These people and supportive associates had become my family of choice, I suppose, in the absence of a complete, older one. The men with whom I suffered, those I had the privilege to help, people everywhere working for honest change, and those in other places who decided to speak truth to power and its corruption, were my future. They were all I had left besides a sister who wrote; a tireless brother Jim; a handful of friends, relatives, and children who remained loyal; and my dear mother.

CHAPTER 39

DEATH IN THE FAMILY

Cherokee Prayer of Purification

Great Spirit, whose voice I hear in the wind,
Whose breath gives life to all the World. Hear me;
I need your strength and wisdom.
Let me walk in beauty, and make my eyes behold the red and
purple sunset.
Make my hands respect the things you have made and my
ears sharp to hear your voice.

Make me always ready to come to you with clean hands and
straight eyes.
So when life fades, as the fading sunset, my spirit may come
to you without shame.

Closing prayer at funeral of Pat Gwyn Woltz,
September 17, 2011

September 14, 2011

Throughout this journey, my mother was always there. She wrote a daily letter. When I did not receive one for three days in mid-September, I worried. Throughout my dark days,

Jim provided every possible financial and physical support, but it was Mother who was my emotional and spiritual support. We spoke on the phone at 8:30 every Saturday morning for thirty-five years, no matter where I lived in the world. She filled me with her daily letters and she filled the prison library with books.

Wednesday, September 14, was her 86th birthday. Acting Camp Administrator Michael J. Snow came to the sweat lodge. Our last song finished, flap of the *inipi* opened, and with the sight of Snow at the fence of our sacred grounds serenity stopped. It is a grueling ritual, and I was exhausted, having run the ceremony, but more bothered by his willingness to interrupt it.

"I hope you have a good reason for this, Mr. Snow."

"Pack your stuff and come with me," and he turned to walk away.

"Why?"

Over his shoulder, he replied, "Attorney Art Strickland just sent you an e-mail. Your mother had a stroke. She's dying."

Snow was monitoring my communications. By the time I got Jim on the phone, Mother was dead. She died in his arms on the way home from the hospital. Through his sorrow, he related her last look, blue orbs twinkling. She smiled, said, "I love you," and closed her eyes forever.

My *outdate* was February 13, 2012, sixteen weeks away. I was cleared for home confinement by U.S. Probation. Mt. Airy, NC, where Mother lived, was only two hours away, and Congresswoman Virginia Foxx offered arrangements to get me there and back for the funeral in one day.

Counselor Canterberry, a defendant in one of my suits, called me to the Administration Office. A request to go to the funeral was already on file with my counselor and case manager. Canterberry's call was worrisome.

As I entered the Administration Office, his boss, Mr. Snow, disappeared. Canterberry stood nose-to-nose with me and screamed, "Your request to go to your mother's funeral has been denied, Woltz! Do you understand me?"

"I don't understand anything about any of you up here, Mr. Canterberry," and walked out, only to be stopped by Snow, who was hiding around the corner.

"Wait a minute, Woltz! Wait a minute! Maybe there is something we can do."

I wasn't about to be provoked into an incident; I knew their tricks. My mother was dead, and I did not feel like playing games.

Snow called Canterberry outside and the counselor apologized, though the incident was obviously his doing. I was expected to react, get loud, and give them an excuse in the presence of the Duty Guard standing inside the door, to send me to the "hole" at the FCI for assaulting an officer, which is defined as little more than loud or abusive language.

Canterberry said, "Maybe I could have handled that a little better."

"I hope one day you gentlemen are in my shoes and have the pleasure of dealing with people like yourselves," I replied and turned to leave.

Snow said, "Wait, wait, Woltz! I'll let you go if we send two armed guards to be there at the funeral. You can go in, stand up front against the wall with them, and they'll bring you back when it's over. How about that?"

Under B.O.P. policy, I was already *community custody* and no guards were required.

"We don't need to discuss it any more, Mr. Snow," I said. "I would not dishonor my mother by having people whom she held in such low regard present at a service in her memory."

The truth of what happened soon came out. The falsification of my work records increased my security rating, though the Code of Federal Regulations stated my status automatically changed to *community custody* in June, the year before, when the warden signed my release paperwork. Case Manager Thomas Carter, Smith's replacement, did not adjust my status. He was also subject of a suit for not following the CFRs (Code of Federal Regulations), which might explain his failure to follow law and policy in my case, but that was his job. The provocation on the day of my mother's death was intended to provide an excuse to refuse my request to attend her funeral, or force me to 'voluntarily' accept a higher security status (and guards) commensurate with it. Because my records were illegally altered and the prison officials failed to grant me the custody status required by their regulations, guards at the funeral would be required to cover their misdeeds. I was improperly and illegally listed as a security risk. Had my mother not died, this would never have come to light.

My own situation highlighted the suit regarding the falsification of prisoner work records. Mr. Marabillas, boss at General Maintenance, never gave me a rating below "excellent" and I was ranked his top, number one, employee. Further, I was payroll clerk and kept copies of my monthly reports as well as those of all other top-ranked workers as evidence for the lawsuit. Case Manager Smith and Counselor Grimes simply falsified our ratings in the prison record to "poor" or "fair," which put us at *out custody*, a higher security rating. That also acted to deny us early release to home confinement, as required by federal law, or such things as going to a family funeral without guards.

Over one thousand people attended the funeral of Pat Gwyn Woltz, artist, mother, and civic leader, but I was not among them. As my childhood friend, Allen Johnson, recently said, "When your mother walked into the room, everybody felt like God just entered as well." Her loving spirit was indeed that strong.

We held a service for Mother at the *inipi* the following week, and I sang the Lakota Death Song to send her to the Spirit World. Her presence was felt by all present. My friend Allen was right. The Great Creator was her Guide and Companion, even in a tent of blankets.

CHAPTER 40

THE FINAL BATTLES AND LAST DAYS

"Sed quis custodient ipsos custodes?"

(But who is to guard the guardians themselves?)

Decimus Junius Juvenal, Roman poet, 1st *and 2*[nd] *century, A.D.*

January 31, 2012

S now informed me two weeks before my official outdate I would not be released unless I signed a contract to go to a *halfway house*. I was already approved for home confinement and scheduled to leave prison on February 13, 2012. Halfway houses are privately owned businesses originally designed to house released prisoners without a home: a worthy purpose. Once established as a profit center in the prison industry, however, all prisoners were forced to go to them in spite of law requiring the opportunity for six months of home confinement. I have yet to see any prisoner receive home confinement since the for-profit halfway house industry took hold.

Released prisoners also now suffer what is known as *supervised release*. Those leaving prison are monitored and restricted for years or life, though their sentence has been completed in full. Parole existed until 1994 when supervised release went into effect during the Clinton Administration. Under the parole system, prisoners were released *before* the completion of sentence, if deemed non-violent with a good record. Supervised release, conversely, restricts the prisoner's liberty for years or life, *after* his or her debt to society has been fulfilled. This only serves the prison industry, not the public's safety or the rights of citizens. The statute states supervised release is to be used sparingly as Congress' intent was that it be used only in cases where the prisoner needed assistance in finding a home, getting a job, or was truly violent, but this law now serves the prison industry instead. Defendants received a post-sentence restriction in every case I have reviewed, making likely their return to prison for any violation. These private halfway houses reputedly pay prison Case Managers quite well to ensure they stay full, though such payments are nothing more than a bribe. My case manager, as example, drove a Hummer; the most expensive automobile in the parking lot.

Halfway houses are a multi-billion dollar industry, and my research led to but one conclusion; they are a fraudulent scheme. I refused to go to one, which had never happened before, according to Acting Camp Administrator Snow. Federal law required me to have six months of "home-confinement" at the end of my sentence, and I intended to get it. I also did not want to be under the Bureau of Prisons supervision when released, as our relationship had been less than cordial. Halfway houses are a private extension of Bureau of Prisons authority, whereas home confinement would place me under the Office of U.S. Probation. I suspected there were those who would gladly return me to prison in retaliation for my filings. Private halfway house owners have both the authority and incentive to do so, as they get repeat business. A U.S. Probation officer has the opposite incentive, which is to lessen his or her workload by seeing that persons who are not a danger to society are off probation as soon as possible.

My cellmate at the time, Randolph Wilson, was returned to FPC-Beckley by his halfway house on five occasions during supervised release, on one conviction. He spent more time in prison on alleged violations of halfway house rules than on his original sentence, though none of those infractions were crimes. This costs the federal government and taxpayers significant sums, while providing no discernable benefit to society.

Snow, having monitored my communications, also knew a documentary was being filmed upon my release. The Director, Cody T. Joel, and his film crew were to be at Vernice's house February 14. Mr. Snow hoped to disrupt those plans by seeing to it I went to a halfway house, whose rules precluded contact with media. Meeting with the film director or a news reporter would be cause for a return trip to prison. Snow was relentless, but I had seen another prisoner, Ryan Featherson of Greensboro, NC, trapped by this scheme after his release. He was interviewed by local TV and sent back to FPC-Beckley within days, though media contact is not against the law and is in fact, a constitutional right, even while in prison. Having witnessed this firsthand, I was alerted to Snow's plan.

By forcing a halfway house stop, even if I did not spend a single night there, Snow could impose those identical rules and Bureau of Prisons' control. Halfway houses are paid a substantial daily fee ranging from $110 to $200, often using old motels and confining four persons per room. State and federal governments pay these exorbitant rates not only for each release day in the halfway house but also after the prisoner goes home. If the Case Manager assigns six months in a halfway house, the government pays for 180 days, even if the person spends but one night. The private business is free to resell the same empty bunk over and again, making these operations enormously profitable, all at taxpayer and prisoners' expense. I estimated at the low end of the rate scale, a halfway house could generate as much as $2,400 each day for a motel room that once rented for $29.95 a night. This number does not include the twenty-five percent of pre-tax income taken from each occupant as part of the contract. I refused to sign Snow's agreement.

The halfway house program works like a scam and accomplishes little for the betterment of the released prisoner or society at-large. Both pay a heavy price. Recently released prisoners should not have an additional quarter of their pre-tax income taken from them. This burden stands to increase the likelihood he or she will take up criminal activity as a matter of survival. America now has the highest rate of recidivism in the world, and I believe that is due largely to our system of post-incarceration *supervised release* combined with halfway houses, which have strong incentives to send citizens back to prison as many times as possible. Since supervised release replaced parole in 1994, prison populations have exploded, along with recidivism. Parole encouraged good behavior and rewarded a prisoner with early release. By releasing those who are not a danger to society in exchange, we all avoid unnecessary expenses, human and financial. The system of probation should be restored. It is smart, and all the incentives are correctly placed. Supervised release, on the other hand, places all incentives in the wrong place and sets tripwires for failure, costing the taxpayer and released prisoner in the process, seemingly all for a profit.

The home confinement I was due under law would put me under the direct control of U.S. Probation rather than the Bureau of Prisons. I would avoid the privately owned halfway house altogether and it would be far more difficult for Snow and others to have me sent back to prison.

Mr. Snow was relentless in his efforts, but I wouldn't go to a halfway house for these reasons and was equally obstinate in refusing. There were daily calls to the Administration Office, promising some new variation of a halfway house contract. He showed me e-mail from the halfway house coordinator for North Carolina, Erlinda Hernandez, saying if I would sign the contract, she would require only a single check in and permit release to home the same day "in all likelihood."

"Mr. Snow, I think I should stay here for another six months and keep you honest. We'll have fun." And that is what we did.

I filed a federal lawsuit against Snow and Case Manager Thomas Carter for violating the law requiring six months home confinement.

The falsification of my work records was their justification. This remained an issue and the basis of a lawsuit in the local federal court two years hence, which was dismissed immediately after my release.

When I filed the new suit on home confinement, a local federal magistrate, reputedly with ties to the prison union, dismissed it under a rule that applies only to cases filed by state prisoners (28 U.S.C. §2254). The Court's ruling stated I must exhaust all remedies in *state* court before I could file in the federal Court. My case was not a state case nor was I a state prisoner, and, therefore, had no standing before a state court. The ruling was a detour to judicial oblivion, intended to ride out the clock. I was already beyond my lawful release date and the court's order was nonsensical. 28 U.S.C. §2254 specifically states that it applies *only* to those convicted *in or by a state court.* The judge's order was so inexplicable I filed a complaint against him with the Fourth Circuit Judicial Review Committee. It was dismissed without addressing the issue, the same outcome of those I filed against Judge Britt.

By that time, I had filed appeals of my conviction from both the district court in the Southern District of West Virginia where I originally filed a *habeas* petition; filed multiple appeals to the Western District of North Carolina; and filed through the Fourth Circuit Court of Appeals, to the Supreme Court on four separate occasions. I proved actual innocence as far back as 2009, but gave up on that issue after Chief Justice John Roberts' decision in *District Attorney's Office for the Third Judicial District et al. v. Osborne* that same year. He ruled "actual innocence" was not a reason for relief. I told my mother about this ruling before she died. She very politely said she did not believe me. She claimed such a ruling could never be made in the United States of America, so I sent her a copy of it. She was right in that it was unbelievable such a decision could be made in this nation, but it was also true that our Supreme Court made it:

'Osborne [the Appellant] also obliquely relies on an asserted federal constitutional right to be released upon proof of "actual innocence." *Whether such a federal right exists is an open question. We have struggled with it over the years, in some cases assuming, arguendo, that it exists while also noting the difficult questions such a right would pose and the high standard any claimant would have to meet.' Decided June 18, 2009, Opinion written by Chief Justice Roberts* [Emphasis added]

The Roberts Court decided there was no right to be released on proof of "actual innocence," indicating, in my opinion, just how far from rule of law and true justice our nation has traveled. If actual innocence is not a cause for release, what is? A court's sole task in criminal matters is to determine guilt or innocence. After reading this ruling, I only challenged issues of jurisdiction and my counsel's ineffectiveness in my appeals, as those were evident from the docket sheet itself and could not be waived by any plea agreement. The laziest of law clerks could see Judge Britt had no authority to remove me from the Western District to his foreign jurisdiction and his rulings were, therefore, void when made. No court should have to "struggle" with that, as Chief Justice John Roberts did with actual innocence. The Court has deemed *technicalities* are still cause for overturn, though actual innocence *is not*, which mystifies me.

The fact that Judge Britt and AUSA Martens so clearly broke the law, I firmly believe, is also the reason no court has ever ruled on these issues or addressed them. My claims are irrefutable from the docket sheet alone. Relief is required to be given by law. Should the court acknowledge Britt and Martens acted outside of their lawful scope and authority, however, that would act to remove their immunity, opening them to suit and possible prosecution. I believe the higher courts refused to rule solely to protect their own until statute of limitations ran. It is not my word against theirs; it is as Art Strickland wrote the Court in Charlotte, "evident just by looking at the docket sheet of Howell's case."

To this date, I have never been convicted in or by any court with the jurisdiction to do so, yet completed an eighty-seven month sentence, while every court with the authority to correct this wrong-doing has turned a blind eye and refused to rule on the merits of my claims or acknowledge the crimes and misdeeds of their peers. The conclusion seems clear. Law no longer applies to those enfranchised to dispense its penalties.

Better to keep an innocent man in prison than admit a senior federal judge and a star-bound Assistant U.S. Attorney broke the law. But I have not and will not give up.

Whether it is in a court of law or the court of public opinion, I will one day be heard.

CHAPTER 41

WALKING OUT THE DOOR A FREE MAN

"To declare that in the administration of criminal law the end justifies the means—to declare that the Government may commit crimes in order to secure the conviction of a private citizen—would bring great retribution."

U.S. Supreme Court Justice, Louis D. Brandeis

August 10, 2012 – FPC-Beckley to Roanoke, VA and freedom

The prison had no lawful choice but to release me on August 10. I served every day of an eighty-seven month sentence unlawfully imposed by Britt's court, but still had little faith I would be released. There was no indication up until that day it was actually going to happen, and I was six months beyond the date of required release to home confinement. I kept uniforms and commissary until my name was called for R & D (Release and Discharge) at 6 a.m. I expected *diesel therapy* or to be further violated by Judge Britt. Several friends came to the cubicle upon hearing the call and helped carry the six boxes of accumulated appeals and lawsuits.

Mr. Ellison at R & D said, "No one ever left prison with that much legal work, Woltz." He found two carts to carry the load to a dark parking lot. My old boss, Tom Marabillas, came to yesterday's sweat lodge ceremony. There was a simple handshake and quiet good-bye in case they did let me go. Ms. Fletcher came by too. A surprising number of guards privately expressed gratitude and wished me well, including some of Grimes' coterie. They appeared to be grateful he was gone. I appreciated their sincerity, but it was a strange, uneasy situation only time can sort out.

Waiting outside were Jim and Jill. I walked unchained towards them but not completely untethered to Mr. Ellison. The Beckley airport was only a half a mile from prison. They flew in that morning so I might have a quick trip home. The short rental car ride to the airport was long enough to leave me queasy. My companions were different, but the experience oddly reminded me of diesel therapy from 2009.

They brought new clothes, which I donned in the airport men's room. Despite the flurry of thoughts and emotions I was overwhelmed by deep gratitude. Through these years, Jim and Jill had provided and cared for me. It was especially evident that day.

The pilot packed the legal files. We boarded and roared down the runway. "Do it," Jim said and his pilot made the turn.

The plane banked north, providing a view of the Camp track. My mind ran through some of the estimated 5,000 miles gathered there as we moved eastward, the buildings below getting smaller along with the memory of having been in them.

I was unable to speak. It was not until the final approach to the Roanoke airport did I realize it was over. We drove directly to their home on Bent Mountain for my first opportunity to meet their twin sons, John and Jacob. By 9 a.m. we were eating a porch breakfast, overlooking the Shenandoah Valley. So much had been missed in the intervening years.

The day's travels and opportunities to express gratitude were not over. The three of us left Bent Mountain for lunch with Art Strickland and his wonderful assistant, Patty Ballard. She had typed the first version of *Justice Denied*. It was my first chance to give direct thanks. We were also met by Jim's equally wonderful assistant, Kelly Kiser, who typed the many letters to David Freedman and the court during my first twenty-four months. Without those records, I could never prove my story true. One doesn't repay this kind of debt, not in the traditional sense anyway

The next day, Jim and I drove to our mother's home in Mt. Airy. The family kept everything exactly as it was the day she died. Upon entering her bedroom I saw Mother's watch, wound and set beside her hairbrush and mirror. Her favorite slippers rested just under the bed. Seven years of tears were allowed to fully flow.

On Sunday, Vernice and our sons arrived. Childhood friend, Allen Johnson, came by too. Chief of Police, Robert Cook, called Jim's cellphone and wanted to know when I would be back in Davie County. Soon enough, I thought with some trepidation.

Vernice and I drove home not knowing each other. In seven years we had become different people. The vicissitudes and vacillations had taken their due toll. I had no idea what the future held for us, though she had promised me she was committed to our marriage in the latest swing of emotion several months prior.

We arrived not at *our* home but her new home. There were no yellow ribbons or signs of welcome. I was shown to the upstairs guest room rather than the master bedroom where she slept. When I touched her, our contact was equally distant. She withdrew.

Twenty-three years of marriage, I soon learned, were over. It had come in sputters and not without warning but several days later, I asked if she had any intention of reviving what had been. The final message, conveyed that day, still stunned. When Chris drove me to what had been our home, the farm, I was heartbroken. I carried $200 from prison and no driver's license but a wish to begin anew after she told me she had long planned to divorce, but waited until my release to tell me. I soon learned the status of my assets; this shocked me more than the divorce. Like the love I thought was still there, they were missing as well.

I first rode a bicycle as the only means of transportation and would later buy my son's Jeep, which some years before, my money had originally purchased for him. New York City removed his need for it. I fully understood the stories and plight of prisoners starting over and wondered how those less fortunate survived. It was a system designed for failure. In my case a stipend from Mother's IRA began the month after my release, otherwise I would have been penniless.

The farmhouse had also not faired well in my absence. Although a hunt club rented the rest of the farm and sent a monthly check to my family, general care and maintenance ended on the old farmhouse when Vernice vacated it. Its only occupants were squirrels living in the ceiling and the boy's bedroom, and snakes that found the chimney. There were remnants of other guests, animal skeletons on the hearth. The entire scene was covered in layers of dust and cobwebs and the 150-year-old hand-hewn beams looked ghostly. The sinks didn't drain and the hot water was cold. One eye on the gas stove worked, but not the oven.

But it was my home, and I would make it so again.

Cleaning and repairing did not seem like work after the heartbreak, but a catharsis. With the disappearance of each layer of residue I felt a joy, a sensation long absent from life. I was engrossed in productive work. I heard tree frogs at night and the call of wild geese by day. These were now new sensations and sounds. They thrilled my soul. I tasted ripe fox grapes, chestnuts and fresh vegetables as if never known childhood delights. The healing view of the pond from the porch, where my children spent their youth, brought the journey full circle, to the memory of fishing together, a day before the arrest, and then backwards through a seven year odyssey of America's system of 'justice.'

An opened closet door displayed the clothes for a man I no longer knew. The attire of a businessman were on display, the assorted custom suits, handmade shoes, silk ties, cuff links, all the accouterment of another day, were not wanted or needed. Had I identified with the clothing mattered not, for nothing fit my lighter frame by fifty pounds.

My new line of work was that of a reformer. I could shed the old skin as the snakes theirs in this same house.

Edmond Hannah, the prison law librarian, once told me his best day in prison could not compare with his worst day of freedom. Mr. Hannah's words often came to mind during those first few months of freedom. I mourned the fact he would not experience the wisdom of his own words. He died the year he was to be released. I might alter his words some and say: The simple joys of living with choice are always better than arbitrary ones mandated by others.

My pleasures abound: planting a fall garden, repairing the old greenhouse, cutting wood for the cabin stove. Life is a good mixture of old and new, the best parts of each making a different whole. And with it came joy and the awakening of a satisfying, unexpected peace.

EPILOGUE

August 10, 2013
It has now been exactly one year since leaving prison.

Shortly after release, I met a wonderful chaplain and fell in love with her. She has worked tirelessly to heal the farmhouse as well as the man who lives in it. Her presence is magical.

I carried far more from prison than just legal files. The emotional baggage and memories have been hard to release. I no longer wake up with nightmares of being pulled from bed and shipped off, but I also know I will never be the same.

It will be a great day when I have no motions to file and no battles to wage, but until then, I intend to fight for a broader and truer system of justice. As Martin Luther King wrote from the Birmingham Jail, "Injustice anywhere, is a threat to justice everywhere." We the People, can collectively choose a different course for our country. To do otherwise will mean our woes will only worsen. The *land of the free and home of the brave* should not have the largest prison population, highest conviction rate, greatest number of agencies with police powers, and most numerous means of imprisoning its citizens than any other nation on earth or in human history.

Change can come if our leaders alter the incentives; reward justice rather than convictions; imprison those we fear rather than those we dislike; hold government to law in equal measure to the citizenry, punishing violators of both; eliminate private trafficking in public punishment; reserve criminal punishment for violations of criminal law; imprison only those who commit *real* crimes: murder, rape, robbery, aggravated assault and intentional fraud *(mala en se)*, rather than for bad behavior *(mala prohibida)*. In short, follow the United States Constitution.

Howell W. Woltz

For story updates on this effort, please visit www.howellwoltz.com or contact me via email: howell@howellwoltz.com.

Justice Denied: The United States v. the People and *The Way Back to America: a 10-Step Plan to Restore the United States to Constitutional Government* are both available on Amazon.com, Barnesandnoble.com, or http://www.justicedenied.com.

To invite Mr. Woltz to speak to your organization, law school or university, contact him at: howell@howellwoltz.com or Howell@WoltzMedia.com

NOTES

W ith only 5% of the world's population, the United States of America has 25% of its prisoners. There are more laws requiring the penalty of prison in the United States than in any other country or in human history. Congress has defined some 14,000 human activities as *criminal* at the federal level alone. Congress has given Executive Branch prosecutors unlimited means to incarcerate the general population, including political targets. Over 10,000 of these laws are *civil* statutes, yet Congress has assigned the *criminal* punishment of prison for their transgression. For the most part, discretionary sentencing has been removed from judges and juries and the power vested in Executive Branch prosecutors through legislatively mandated sentences under the *U.S. Sentencing Guidelines.* The net effect is the politicization of American justice.

Over 18,000 separate police agencies now exist in our nation, each with the authority to enforce these 14,000 laws. It is doubtful any tyrant has been imbued with the same statistical powers, nor has any police state in history possessed such means of subjugating its citizenry. These numbing figures alone should act as a wake-up call. I was unaware of our nation's course until government misapplied these assumed powers in my case. I view this as tyrannical and a particular threat to younger citizens. Boston attorney and author, Harvey Silverglate, estimated each of us unknowingly averages three transgressions of federal law a day. Cicero said, "The more laws, the less justice." I concur. With enough laws, anyone can be targeted and imprisoned. Some of the more egregious and aggressively applied are the *conspiracy* laws. One man's notion of applied safety is another man's prison term. These laws must find their way to the dustbin of history before our nation can hope to return to one of law and true justice.

The conviction rate in our Federal courts is 98.6%. This is an appallingly high rate, one obtainable only by denying citizens the very legal protections our Constitution affords. An indictment in America statistically results in a sentence. Should we not ask of ourselves and our elected leaders from all levels of government why this has happened, and how these mistakes can be corrected? The overwhelming majority of the14,000 behaviors criminalized by Congress appear to be outside of its constitutional authority. Judges and justices, prosecutors and agents of law enforcement, too often act as if innocence no longer matters and Constitutional rights are merely electives, subject to their whim. We lack sufficient means to remove them when they violate law and Constitution themselves. It is now our duty to act, as the proprietors of this nation, to advocate meaningful change and help public servants, elected and otherwise, take us out of the abyss.

Howell W. Woltz

October 17, 2013

SPECIAL THANKS

A very special thanks to Rob Calvert, whom I have the honor and privilege of knowing as a brother-in-law, but consider a brother. Not only is his original work displayed on the cover (*The Homefront*), the cover itself was his design and doing.

Rob then laboriously reviewed and recommended changes to what went between the book's cover to help wring out much of the cynicism and anger that still came through in my writing. It is a far better tome in every respect thanks to Rob's patient input and assistance, for which I am grateful.

Howell Woltz
October 23, 2013

APPENDIX: PRISON MOVES

I was moved a total of twenty-nine times between jails and prisons carrying me as far west as Oklahoma, as far north as upstate New York, and as far south as the Georgia/Florida line. By law, I could only be moved from the Charlotte Division of the Western District to prison in West Virginia, and only after being convicted in that Court and District, which never occurred. These were wrongful acts intended to punish me excessively and inhumanly. They constituted torture by any normal standard. In prison it's known as **'diesel therapy'**.

The month before my first scheduled sentencing hearing I was moved to various detention centers. I was in Atlanta less than 24 hours before being moved to Wilson, NC, Louisburg, NC, back to Charlotte, and back to Raleigh with various stops in between. (Actual sentencing was October 2. 2007.) I filed a Motion to be returned to the Western District.

Immediately following sentencing, I was taken to Western Tidewater Jail located in Suffolk, VA. I had no access to telephone or law, which meant I was not able to file a Direct Appeal within the time limit. I was there 10/01/2007 to 12/25/2007. The next stop was Oklahoma for two months.

After arriving at Beckley in February, 2008 I immediately began filing appeals for myself and others. I worked on 300 plus cases to help fellow inmates get their sentences reduced. I was known as 'the jail house lawyer'. I also filed numerous suits against prison guards and officials who were violating prisoners' rights. The prison system retaliated by sending me on tours around the country. The object was to deny me access to law and court.

APPENDIX: PRISON MOVES

Jail / Prison Moves During Time of Confinement
(April, 2006 – August, 2012)

Jail/Prison Moves During Time of Confinement (April, 2006 - August, 2012)

	Transfer Origin	Origin Judicial District	Destination	Destination Judicial District	Reason for Move	Detention Facility	Dates Approximate	Transport Method
1	Davie County	Middle	Charlotte, NC	Western	Court Order - Judge Keesler	Meck. Cnty Jail	04/18/06	Western District FBI
2	Charlotte, NC	Western	Raleigh, NC	Eastern	Court Order - Judge Britt	Wake Cnty Jail	04/22/06	U.S. Marshal
3	Raleigh, NC	Eastern	Charlotte, NC	Western	Unknown	Meck. Cnty Jail	04/25/06	U.S. Marshal
4	Charlotte, NC	Western	Raleigh, NC	Eastern	Court Order - Judge Britt	Wake Cnty Jail	10/01/06	U.S. Marshal
5	Raleigh, NC	Eastern	Charlotte, NC	Western	Unknown	Meck. Cnty Jail	10/04/06	U.S. Marshal
6	Charlotte, NC	Western	Raleigh, NC	Eastern	Court Order - Judge Britt	Wake Cnty Jail	02/05/07	U.S. Marshal
7	Raleigh, NC	Eastern	Charlotte, NC	Western	Unknown	Meck. Cnty Jail	02/08/07	U.S. Marshal
8	Charlotte, NC	Western	Atlanta, GA		Unknown	U.S. Penitentiary, Atlanta, GA	05/07/07	Bureau of Prisons
9	Atlanta, GA		Wilson, NC	Eastern	Unknown	Wilson Cnty. Jail	05/08/07	Bureau of Prisons
10	Wilson, NC	Eastern	Charlotte, NC	Western	Unknown	Meck. Cnty Jail	June/2007	Sheriff
11	Charlotte, NC	Western	Louisburg, NC	Eastern	Unknown	Franklin Cnty Jail	June/2007	Sheriff
12	Louisburg, NC	Eastern	Raleigh, NC	Eastern	Unknown	Wake Cnty Jail	June/2007	Sheriff
13	Raleigh, NC	Eastern	Charlotte, NC	Western	Court Order - Judge Britt	Meck. Cnty Jail	June/2007	U.S. Marshal
14	Charlotte, NC	Western	Raleigh, NC	Eastern	Court Order - Judge Britt	Wake Cnty Jail	07/07/07	U.S. Marshal
15	Raleigh, NC	Eastern	Charlotte, NC	Western	Unknown	Meck. Cnty Jail	07/11/07	U.S. Marshal
16	Charlotte, NC	Western	Raleigh, NC	Eastern	Court Order - Judge Britt	Wake Cnty Jail	09/30/07	U.S. Marshal
17	Raleigh, NC	Eastern	Western Tidewater Regional Jail	State of Virginia	Unknown	Suffolk, VA	10/01/07	U.S. Marshal
18	Western Tidewater Regional Jail	Virginia	Oklahoma City Federal Transfer Center	Oklahoma	Unknown	Beckley Federal Prison, Beaver, WV	02/07/08	Prison Air Transport Service

APPENDIX: PRISON MOVES

Jail / Prison Moves During Time of Confinement (April, 2006 – August, 2012)

	Transfer Origin	Origin Judicial District	Destination	Destination Judicial District	Reason for Move	Detention Facility	Dates Approximate	Transport Method
19	Beckley Prison	West Virginia	Atlanta, GA	Georgia	Unknown	Atlanta United States Prison	4/16/2009	Prison Air Transport Service
20	Atlanta United States Prison	Georgia	Oklahoma City, OK	Oklahoma	Unknown	Oklahoma City Federal Transfer Center, via Memphis, TN & Kansas City	4/17/2009	Prison Air Transport Service
21	Oklahoma City Federal Transfer Center	Oklahoma	Chickasha, OK	Oklahoma	Unknown	Grady County Jail	4/17/2009	Sheriff
22	Grady County Jail	Oklahoma	Oklahoma City, OK	Oklahoma	Unknown	Oklahoma City Federal Transfer Center	4/24/2009	Sheriff
23	Oklahoma City Federal Transfer Center	Oklahoma	Charlotte, NC	Western District, NC	Unknown	Meck. Cnty Jail, via Indiana, New York & Philadelphia	4/24/2009	Prison Air Transport Service
24	Meck. Cnty Jail	Western District, NC	Ocilla, GA	Georgia	Unknown	Irwin Cnty Detention Center	8/24/2009	Sheriff
25	Irwin Cnty Detention Center	Georgia	Atlanta, GA	Georgia	Unknown	Atlanta United States Prison	8/26/2009	Sheriff
26	Atlanta United States Prison	Georgia	Oklahoma City, OK	Oklahoma	Unknown	Oklahoma City Federal Transfer Center	8/27/2009	Prison Air Transport Service
27	Oklahoma City Federal Transfer Center	Georgia	Chickasha, OK	Oklahoma	Unknown	Grady County Jail	8/27/2009	Sheriff
28	Grady County Jail	Oklahoma	Oklahoma City, OK	Oklahoma	Unknown	Oklahoma City Federal Transfer Center	8/29/2009	Sheriff
29	Oklahoma City Federal Transfer Center	Oklahoma	Beaver, WV	West Virginia	Unknown	Beckley Federal Prison, Beaver, WV	8/29/2009	Prison Air Transport Service

Made in the USA
Lexington, KY
14 April 2014